Barcode Tattoo
Poetry in parkrun

Roger G McDonald

Barcode Tattoo

www.rogergmcdonald.com
ISBN: 978-0-9873563-3-8
Author: Roger G McDonald
Cover design and typesetting: Sandy McDonald
Copyright: ©Roger G McDonald 2022

All rights reserved. No part of *Barcode Tattoo* may be reproduced, stored in a retrieval system, or transmitted in any form or by any means without the prior permission of the author.

LEGAL NOTICE

While all reasonable attempts have been made to verify information provided in this book, neither the author nor the publisher assumes any responsibilities for errors, omissions, or contradictory information contained in *Barcode Tattoo*.

The author and publisher make no representation or warranties with respect to the accuracy, applicability, fitness or completeness of the contents of *Barcode Tattoo*.

The author specifically disclaims any liability directly or indirectly which is incurred as a consequence, directly or indirectly, of the use and application of any contents of this work.

Dedication

This book is dedicated to parkrunners the world over, and especially the volunteers who make a great idea grand.

A special mention to the event team, volunteers, and participants of Coburg parkrun in Melbourne, Australia. Logic says you're no different to any of the thousands of parkrun communities across the globe. They bring joy, companionship, and hope wherever they function.

In Coburg parkrun's case, their consistently enthusiastic welcome to all-comers, and particularly first-time attendants and tourists, gave this book its impetus. More, it helped maintain the faith through the long days of COVID-19 lockdowns when I wrote some of this work.

ACKNOWLEDGEMENT

Once again, my wife, Sandy McDonald, has excelled in making sense of the shambles I presented her.

She has turned this into a work of art as only she can.

Contents

Dedication and acknowledgement	iii
Contents	iv
Foreword: Paul Sinton-Hewitt CBE, FRS	8
Introduction	11
CHAPTER 1: Origins. Is this tattoo for life?	**13**
Barcode Tattoo	25
Sub 25:00	26
Category of one	27
Hamstrung	28
Coburg molehill	30
Democracies of distance	33
Sodbridge	34
Ghost of Hillary	37
Amateur pentameter	38
Discomfort zones	39
Spaced out on statistics	40
Running out of taxes	43
Countdown to sub 24:00	44
A run for all seasons	46
Summer	46
Autumn	46
Winter	47
Spring	47
Smart money	48
Newtrition	50
The rogue	51
Pop guns and top guns	53
Stopwatch conspiracy	54
Battles with the lizard	57
Sighcology	59
Quick questions for slow runners	60
First timers	61
Last shuffle	63

Making up the numbers	65
Time was a war	66
Forgot-me-knot	67
Blood running	68
Chariots of childhood	71
Rain	72
Wind	72
Smoke	73
Snow	73
Heat	75
Sweat	75
Humidity	76
Sand	76
Top ten	77
A ton of running	78
CHAPTER 2: Volunteers. Winners come last.	**81**
Winners come last	84
The finish without an end	86
Running out of sight	87
Hymn of the parkrun marshal	88
At the end	89
Cone man	90
The tailer's test	92
CHAPTER 3: Stories. Redemption through laughter and tears.	**93**
Dream of freedom	102
The original Zambezi park run	103
Each shared second	106
Unofficial coach	108
Motion in poetry	109
Gallop poll	110
How to beat Mona the marathoner	112

Contents

CHAPTER 4: Expansion. Running round the world.	**113**
Behind the parkrun curtain	115
Great, Britain!	116
Long road to Canada	117
Time machine	118
Copenhagen	119
Fine footings in France	120
Flying Finns	121
Ode to German joy	122
Torn in the USA	123
See how they run	124
Garibaldi and my red shirt	126
Two Bushy Parks	128
Socrates does parkrun	129
Ireland, a homecoming	130
Eswatini, a kingdom for a course	131
Holding a torch for Japan	132
Fantasia in Malaysia	133
Under Namibia's sun	134
Back from the brink	135
Poland proves a point	136
Kiwi dream	137
Who puts the Eden into Sweden?	138
Foreverland in the Netherlands	139
High lights of Norway	140
Sing a song of Singapore	141
Zimbabwe and the politics of running	142
Running around Afghanistan	144
Auden in Iceland	146

CHAPTER 5: Tourism. Welcome, strangers.	149
Welcome, strangers	150
Henry V at Darebin	151
Caught on the hop	152
Sonnet for Florence	155
Farewell to Florence	156
To beauty and to Bright	157
Happy for Lorne	161
CHAPTER 6: Technology. Don't forget your barcode.	163
Photophalia	164
Technical issues	165
CHAPTER 7: Pandemic. COVID-19 and running on the spot.	167
COVID closure	169
Save your breath	170
Back from the dead	171
The Covid Chronicles	172
CHAPTER 8: Future. Can yesterday ever return to tomorrow?	175
Retreat, not defeat	177
Double negative	178
Run for all, all for the run	180
Index of titles	182
Index of first lines	184
About Roger G McDonald	190
Other works by Roger G McDonald	191
You, parkrun, and the simple gift of soap	192

Foreword

A poetic publishing partnership with parkrun

Paul Sinton-Hewitt CBE, FRSA, founder of parkrun

When we launched what would become parkrun on October 2 2004, we had no idea it would blossom into a global movement that would transform millions of lives.

The initial concept was, and remains, simple. We looked to establish a regular, reliable, measured and timed five kilometre (3.1 mile) event open to all, regardless of age, gender, fitness, or affiliation. Vitally, volunteers should run it in their local communities, and it should be free to all.

In the beginning we hoped a few stalwart runners would turn out, attracted by the promise of a free, regular, weekly event. A few did, fortunately, but the numbers grew slowly.

As we expanded to a second and a third location, we began to think about a name that could work for a larger number of events, and was available online. Participant feedback also told us that our original name might have limitations. The notion of a time trial, while familiar to a range of sporting events, might actually discourage many potential runners, joggers, and walkers. Some perceived it as an event reserved for elite athletes or members of clubs restricted to paid members.

After research and testing, the name parkrun emerged as a viable URL. An unexpected bonus came with it: parkrun clearly, memorably, and universally described the event wherever it took place on the planet. Perhaps like the idea itself, the name parkrun was pre-destined to take its place in the history not just of running, but of active human communities.

A worldwide team of professional experts and enthusiastic volunteers has taken parkrun to their hearts. Not in our most fanciful visions could we have conceived a time when twenty two countries (and counting), thousands of communities, and millions of people would adopt parkrun as an expression of physical and mental well-being.

This same team has meticulously measured and continues to monitor parkrun's effectiveness. They offer advice and suggestions for constant improvement. I'm humbly grateful that the original pillars of the parkrun idea remain as solid today as when they started: a weekly, timed and measured, volunteer-led event free to everyone forever.

In 2014, Debra Bourne's seminal book, *parkrun: much more than just a run in the park*, captured the essence and the history of our movement to date. It did an enormous amount to spread a universal message.

Every week in every country and at every location, tales of courage, generosity, and humour pour in.

And now, with his book, *Barcode Tattoo*, writer, poet, and runner, Roger G McDonald, has given us and the running world something unique.

Barcode Tattoo is special enough for being dedicated entirely to parkrun. Even more compelling is its format: it's written mostly in verse.

Poetry, as many critics point out, is for anyone; it's just not for everyone. But in *Barcode Tattoo*, you'll find works that appeal to every taste as it covers the entire spectrum of all that parkrun stands for.

You could be anyone: a newcomer to running, a junior feeling your way into sport, a parent, a person with a disability determined to overcome a physical or mental well-being issue, a seasoned athlete, or a dog-owner keen to take pooch for a walk.

Just as parkrun has something for everyone, these poems, and their prose companion pieces, are in turn funny, poignant, inspiring, lyrical, energetic, and moving in ways you would rarely expect of poetry.

Just as importantly for parkrun, Roger has generously offered us a publishing partnership. Every book sold contributes to maintaining our most important principle: free for everyone, forever.

I urge you to buy and enjoy *Barcode Tattoo*, and pass the news on to family and friends. If it doesn't get you parkrunning, it might at least get you thinking.

Paul Sinton-Hewitt CBE, FRSA

Introduction

A bit like asking what is the world's most deadly animal to humans*, the puzzle I'm about to put to you is something of a trick question.

If I asked you what is the world's most popular active pastime, a majority—possibly by a considerable margin—would probably nominate football (or soccer so as not to offend exponents of various oval ball codes.)

The image is universal, the reality global. You see them in dusty villages in remote Africa, and jungle clearings in South America; in village squares, and refugee camps, and back lanes, and crowded streets the world over: people kicking a round ball amongst themselves.

Let's pause for a moment, though. Long before any child learns to kick or throw a ball, it first has to find its feet. To parents' frequent alarm, it's soon anxious to extend that proudly earned skill to something altogether more adventurous.

Although it's impossible to measure, I'll stick my neck out and say the true answer to the world's most practised activity is walking, jogging, and running. I believe they surpass every other pursuit we engage in for health and well-being, both physical and mental.

Is it because running is an instinctive form of physical response? Was it instilled in our genes over millennia to activate our fight or flight reaction? Or is it simply the next step after walking to lever our increasingly obese bodies off the couch and away from our screens?

Books, studies, and theses abound on the physiology and psychology of exercise. Many major sports stars (and probably too many minor ones) pen or have biographers write their stories for better or for worse. Is there room in the world for another one on—of all things—the simple act of putting one foot in front of the other?

I was named after Sir Roger Bannister, the first athlete on record to run a sub-four-minute mile. For decades up to and just beyond the Second World War, the feat was thought impossible.

As a tiny mite whose mother was paralysed by multiple sclerosis, domestic responsibilities fell on me and my older siblings sooner and heavier than most.

One of them required me to run to the corner shop for occasional essentials not covered by the weekly expedition to grocer, baker, green grocer, or butcher. Though no more than thirty or forty metres, the dash in the dark was both terrifying and exhilarating.

And the poetry? It too has been a constant companion since childhood. My early exposure to the music and canon of religion incubated a slow-to-fade sense of the numinous. My older sister inflamed a precocious interest in reading. It led to a vivid imagination, which an inspired teacher fed further. His love of English rescued me from a despairing incompetence at just about everything else.

Writing has been my purpose from my early years. As a poet, journalist, and business writer, it has sustained me artistically and financially all my professional life. I hope these words devoted to parkrun bring you enjoyment, and perhaps deepen your appreciation of a movement that has changed the lives of millions.

---

* To answer the question in the opening sentence: the anopheles mosquito. The World Health Organisation estimates deaths from malaria in 2019 totalled 409,000. Children under the age of five years made up 67 per cent of that number.

CHAPTER 1

Origins. Is this tattoo for life?

Tattoos are supposed to last a lifetime. Most are meaningful, at least at the time they're inked in. Some become embarrassing. Falling out of love with a person or a belief or an idea leaves you with a painfully etched or blush-worthy reminder of a failed relationship.

The tattoo at the heart of this book also represents a relationship. It's not between one person and their lover, goal, or ideal, but for millions around our planet and the pursuit of physical and mental wellness. But what is there new to write about an instinct that has driven us since our ancestors dwelt in caves and used their running skills to hunt prey and escape becoming prey?

And if you did have something novel to say, or at least a different way to talk about it, why choose a supposed dinosaur of the language—poetry—to express it?

If you took the number of runners as a percentage of the earth's population, the total would be comparatively low. Yet it appeals to many, as attendances at fun runs and more serious events show globally.

As an international phenomenon, parkrun tells us running,

jogging, and walking appeal to millions within its own ranks. Indeed, among its many other achievements, parkrun may give us a more accurate yet diverse platform on which to guesstimate the number of genuine runners worldwide. But you would have to start with the big qualifying question, a question on which almost nobody with an interest in the subject can agree. Exactly what, or who, is a runner?

Is she the panicked commuter stumbling after her bus or train? The New Year resolutionary puffing for a day or two on the pavement or the treadmill? The solitary, sweat-streaked stick-figures on their quest to find, or perhaps lose themselves?

Another probing question: who is not a runner but qualifies for full membership of the parkrun fellowship? The answer is as broad as the individuals and communities to which parkrun appeals.

Perhaps they're a parent with a child in a pram or pusher; a person with an illness looking to change their life; people with mental health issues in search of companionship and re-affirmation; blind or vision impaired participants who know parkrun will find them a guide; parents, guardians, and grandparents anxious to expand their young charges' horizons with an outdoors challenge diverting them from devices and screens; wheelchair athletes determined to convert a disability into an achievement; prisoners wanting to cling to or rebuild a vestige of a social norm; dog owners and dog lovers delighting in their pets' excitement. And millions more.

If you're reading this, the chances are you may have pondered such questions. You may be a parkrunner, or have one in your family or circle of friends. Consider yourself lucky.

parkrun: *much more than just a run in the park*

Debra Bourne, in her magisterial book *parkrun: much more than just a run in the park,* provides a richly readable account of the birth and growth of parkrun. She gives us its provenance and history, to be sure. But she goes a great deal further, revealing in detail the structure, philosophy, and future of what can now truly be called a worldwide movement.

Bourne lists what have come to be known as 'the pillars of parkrun'—an accurately measured and timed weekly five kilometre event, administered by volunteers, aimed at the inclusive heart of any community, and free to all.

Her primary dedication is praise for the vision of parkrun founder, Zimbabwe-born Englishman, Paul Sinton-Hewitt CBE, FRSA, and his desire to create an inclusive exercise and well-being experience for everyone, not just the elite of an exclusive runners' circle.

Bourne traces the progress of parkrun from its foundation event on October 2 2004 outside London, to the early years of its international expansion. Denmark came aboard in 2009, followed by Australia, Poland, and South Africa in 2011. New Zealand, the United States, Ireland, Russia and Singapore followed in rapid succession.

She also records short-lived events of the era, describing the very first parkrun outside the UK. It took place in embattled Harare, Zimbabwe in 2008 before the idea of parkrun as a global innovation had even arisen.

Although it ran successfully for a couple of years, the weight of political and economic history proved too much even for something as joyous as parkrun.

On a personally poignant note, it reminded me of my eight years in that beautiful but tormented land. Sadly, corruption, greed, and violence have crushed the smiling, sweet-natured aspirations of a peace-loving people.

At the same time, it unearthed memories of an amusing run of my own in a Zimbabwean national park in the wild and remote Zambezi Valley. The occasion could have resulted in disaster but luckily for me ended in farce. (See *The original Zambezi park run* on page 103).

Bourne recounts the set-up of the Iceland event in 2011, importing runners from Denmark and Britain to launch it. After 32 valiant episodes the severe conditions froze it to a close.

Perhaps the most remarkable of the 'temporary' parkruns she recalls was the Camp Bastion event in Afghanistan. Organised by a lance corporal in the British armed forces, the parkrun was 'open to runners of every age, nationality, rank, cap badge, and civilian contractor'. As Britain's military engagement in Afghanistan evolved, the Camp Bastion parkrun slowly wound down, concluding in January 2014 on a very English Nelson—111 events.

From elite Olympians to non-runners

From Olympians such as Sir Mo Farrah, and elite athletes like Australia's Steve Moneghetti to the elderly, people with physical and mental health issues, juniors, and non-runners, Bourne sings a subtle but praiseworthy hymn to an initiative that is equally welcoming and encouraging to all.

Bourne also devotes a chapter to the lifeblood of the universal parkrun phenomenon, the volunteers.

Each parkrun has a trained Event Director responsible for administering the run according to parkrun guidelines. The Event Director organises a team of volunteers who look after different components of the run. The roles include marking out the course in advance for new runners and visitors, marshalling participants safely around the course, photography, timing, distributing finishing tokens, scanning barcodes, and posting results online. The guidelines are simple, but every run follows them to the letter, and for good reason. They set a trusted framework and expectation for parkrunners anywhere on earth.

Each event in parkrun's thousands of locations (and counting) has its own unique and irrepressible identity. But by sticking to the basics—the parkrun pillars—every event gives participants a collective confidence. The consistency, reach, and universality of contemporary online communications mean regular parkrunners, parkrun tourists, and newcomers alike share a known and predictable experience. They know they can roam the planet and find a welcoming parkrun that always follows the same format.

A tattoo for life

Like a tattoo, a once-only online registration assigns every parkrunner their own unique barcode for life. parkrunners carry their barcodes with pride. They arrive for scanning on crumpled scraps of paper, engraved on a car-key disc, laced onto a running shoe, or on parkrun-branded silicon wrist bands. It would come as no surprise to find the odd parkrun devotee sporting their barcode as an actual tattoo for life. No parkrunner worthy of the name finishes an event without it.

No matter where they participate on earth, the parkrun system quickly and accurately records their results. It then upgrades their personal profile across a raft of statistical measurements and publishes it online within hours, sometimes minutes of completion.

Bourne's book also covers other vital components that make parkrun a truly unique phenomenon on the 21st century's honour board of social, community, and sporting successes. She examines the:
- evolution of the technology behind the events
- attraction for families to attend parkrun together
- organic development of shorter junior events
- narrowing of the gulf between traditional running clubs and parkrun as the unorthodox newcomer
- positive effects of recognition, reward, and celebration as participants at all levels work their way towards parkrun milestones
- embrace of parkrun as a community health initiative by councils,

- health authorities, and sponsors keen to see the movement's continued expansion
- tales of adversity, courage, the unexpected, mishaps, and challenges that have tested various parkrun events around the world
- steps required for anyone to set up a new local event
- future of parkrun for its millions of participants.

The parkrun contradiction

Its peculiarity is a contradiction—the bigger it gets, the smaller it becomes. How does that work?

As it grows ever larger internationally, it connects more and more people collectively, locally, and individually. The bond works on two fronts. It imparts the sense of your belonging to an entity much larger than yourself, while remaining an organisation that recognises and celebrates your unique individuality.

It also allows relationships to form and intimacies to be shared based on common joy and mutual encouragement. People have begun to reconnect; to remember how to talk to each other, as well as like, tweet, and friend in the sometimes hollow gloom of digital darkness.

The phenomenon that is parkrun has millions of stories. Comparatively few emerge to the world's eyes each week. But month by month and year by year as event and participant numbers build, the narratives deepen and diversify. Tales of courage, humour, cooperation, collaboration, redemption, recovery, and discovery, abound. The curative effect spreads.

Many of these stories have sad beginnings, and a few, sad endings. But even these—perhaps especially these—begin to show us another side of ourselves. As parkrun spreads beyond its anglosphere origins, the cultural variety of experiences and narratives multiplies.

The mortar that binds them is the enduring promise of the parkrun pillars. It has become an international mantra once spoken only by a few elite runners. Among that small cohort were those few who knew the idea contained a message for the world.

The jovial abbreviation DFYB (Don't forget your barcode!) now unites millions in a kind of irreverent Saturday worship. They carry their parkrun barcodes like a proud tattoo that both identifies them with a collective movement and measures their uniqueness.

Stumbling across parkrun

All the best running manuals, coaches, and serious athletes extol the merits of a running diary. I'm not sure scribbling notes on times, distances, routes, diets, weather, stretches, and all the other mental and physical paraphernalia that goes with running has helped me perform any faster, further, or easier.

But my running diary has performed one significantly useful function. It pinpoints Saturday August 6 2016 as the day I stumbled across a phenomenon that had crept up on us without our realising it; a phenomenon that changed my way of thinking, living, and writing.

The entry that day recorded the usual mechanical details: a 6:30am start to avoid breaking into family weekend time. It noted a chilly six degrees Celsius on the thermometer, overcast skies and—a blessing for a runner of my strictly average talents—no wind. My journal warmed to the notion of perfect conditions to tackle a training target I'd only rarely reached in the last 20 years.

Most regular marathon runners concede the race demands persistence, courage, and … time. They acknowledge the event is a two-act play: performance preceded by preparation. Tough as the 42.2 kilometres is, the thousands of kilometres in training and conditioning represent the hidden bulk of the iceberg.

My goal that August day was, by marathon standards, a relatively modest 25k. Part of the effort took me into new territory in the northern suburbs of my home city of Melbourne, Australia. An

essentially suburban space with a population then of 4.5 million, the city enjoys the good fortune of a network of creeks and interlinking greenbelts. Recent decades have seen local councils and residents' groups engage in increasingly focused efforts to rehabilitate natural waterways. Creeks and lakes that historically were toxic conduits for sewerage and industrial waste are beginning to enjoy a remarkable recovery. With it come walking, running, and cycling tracks in growing numbers and lengths.

The final stages of my run took me along the banks of the Merri Creek. The stream flows through a former bluestone quarry that once provided the material for the forbidding but now decommissioned 1851 bluestone Pentridge prison nearby. A weir dams the creek forming a picturesque reservoir as the centrepiece of Coburg Lake Reserve. The park offers visitors a pleasant green space, with a children's playground and picnic facilities. It teems in the warmer months with families and social groups of every shade and nationality.

Gulping a quick drink at a water fountain, I idly noticed a cluster of people in exercise gear. I took them for a fitness workout group and carried on, intent on navigating through my own joy and pain.

The following Saturday, with no apparent ill effects from my 25k effort, I pushed for a ten per cent increase in distance and time. Repeating the previous route, I set off earlier and extended my run further north. Returning to the same drink stop at the lake, my body and my running watch told me I'd already passed my 27.5k target. By now more familiar with the territory, I knew I had three kilometres to reach home. My diary quotes me muttering through gritted teeth 'You can do this!' 'This' meant running beyond the three hour and 30k barrier.

Again, out of the corner of my eye, I noticed a clot of exercisers. Did I also notice a pennant fluttering in the ice-edged breeze? Or that some of the group wore hi-viz fluorescent vests? My diary doesn't capture it, but my memory does.

The gradual improvement in training consistency and distances produced an inevitable effect. I had to test myself in races. Again.

Over the next eight months, I intermittently searched online for road races and fun runs. Among the many familiar events that had become a part of my racing routine, I came across notices for something called parkrun. It seemed to promote random events in locations around Australia. As a writer and editor I raised a weary eyebrow at the absence of an upper case P, especially at the start of a sentence.

As a younger distance runner, I'd gazed for years at the myth-shrouded Everest of running, the marathon. But more than a decade of travelling in New Zealand, working in the UK, and forging a career and family in the middle of an African civil war took priority.

Serious running would have to wait until I returned with my family to Australia from the shambles of post-independence Zimbabwe. I finally conquered the marathon in Melbourne in 1990, the first of five. Before that, I'd run countless 10 and 15k events and half marathons in training and races.

The parkrun promotions mentioned a free, weekly, measured and timed, volunteer-administered five kilometre event. Even at a low ebb of fitness, five kilometres seemed hardly worth the effort for a race. But inquisitiveness got the better of me. Casual online research took me further into the parkrun story.

Discovering it had become an international phenomenon, I also learned a local event had started up in May 2015 just a few kilometres from home. More from neighbourhood curiosity than any burning desire, I decided to try it once. If nothing else, it would give me an accurate measure of my performance over a measured five kilometre course. And I'd escape the tedium of running and counting laps on a track to check my progress.

Barcode tattoo

We share a passport like a striped tattoo
Whose zebra lines trap time with every scan.
It tells us we are many, yet still few.

The thud of every runner's pounding shoe
Creates the grammar of a world-wide plan:
To share a passport like a striped tattoo.

At first glance we appear a motley crew:
The child, the woman, the pram, the dog, the man.
They tell us we are many, yet still few.

We walk, we jog, we run. Can we outdo
Ourselves? The answer reaffirms: 'We can.'
We share a passport like a striped tattoo.

The passport is our barcode saying who
We are uniquely in the parkrun clan.
It tells us we are many, yet still few.

Unique in person, yet we're married to
An idea with a single global span:
To share a passport like a striped tattoo,
And know we are so many, not so few.

Sub 25:00

Sub 25:00! Your mantra and nirvana
On 5k slogs around a friendly park.
Tormentor, tease, mistress, devil, charmer;
That goal on weekdays seems a simple lark.
Come Saturday, it drags you through a dark

And shattered disillusionment where clocks
Conspire with their grim arithmetic
To ram the message home: Pull up your socks.
You train, run hills, bend, stretch, try every trick.
Your socks and you are stuck at 26:00.

Endorphins conquer too-ambitious blues.
When large, small, young, old, girl, and boy exchange
Those parkrun smiles of shared sweat, you excuse
Today's poor performance, and vow to change.
Sub 25:00 is back within your range!

Category of one

Some Saturdays, my email pats my back.
By late morning, the parkrun volunteers
Have analysed our efforts. My attack
On maybe one more PB soon appears.
Not every run's a record. That's too much
For all self-racers, even the elite.
Still, I've managed to chase down my small clutch
Of stopwatch milestones, though I'll never beat
The whole field in that tough surge for the line.
But how's this! I'm almost undefeated
In my age group. While I'm past my prime,
An ancient's guilt says it's time I tweeted
Why I've won in nearly every run.
I'm mostly in a category of one!

Hamstrung

How many body parts can let you down
On something simple like your weekly run,
And leave you looking like athletics' clown
While feeling that your parkrun's come undone?
Injustice seems to triumph over fun.

The hamstring is today's misdemeanour.
Your form is strong and there's the finish line.
Just one last sprint is all that stands between a
New PB and you, should you incline.
You're fine, but Mister Hammy shrieks: 'Decline!'

Your injured pride is left to hobble through.
But rest, ice, compression, and exercise,
Remind you there is something you can do
To even up the balance, tendon-wise.
An all-walked parkrun? Let's try that for size.

Coburg molehill

A mist rises chilled off the surface.
The ducks and the swans paddle round
The dam where our volunteers service
parkrunners on Saturday's ground.
The wall that holds back the torrent
Spills noisily after a rain.
I guess it delivers its warrant
Of muffling suffering and pain.

The Merri Creek track guides us south
On its gentle trajectory to
Its kiss with the big river's mouth.
There's scarcely a sign of life too,
Just the bush and the birds, plus the snakes
That sensibly stay out of sight.
Survival insists on its high stakes.
We run; and they smartly sit tight.

Origins. Is this tattoo for life?

I start at a clip with the plan my
Momentum will carry me through.
On this course, it's only a stand-by;
Something more than momentum must do
The work on the hill in the back straight
As I trudge up the slope by the lake.
My finish downhill's always too late.
The molehill has made me a fake.

What is it about this strange parkrun
In semi-industrial Coburg?
At times it's the child of the Dark One,
With the wintry soul of an iceberg
Tormenting me from the Antarctic;
And in summer, all desert and heat.
But somehow, it makes my old heart tick.
Without it, no week-end's complete.

Democracies of distance

You count the leaders until you make your turn.
With half the run complete, you can discern
Anxiety on faces yet to reach
The half way mark. You read the hope on each.
You note the contrasts: age, and sex, and size.
Later, the parkrun stats tell truthful lies.
Of course they must report on fleet-foot youth,
And me at war with ruthless senior truth.
But those maths never give a heartening hint
Of how I ran, that lung-scorched, last gasp sprint,
Only to have a ten year old float past
Who, 2ks back, was sure to finish last.
Democracies of a shared distance seem
Bizarre, but they define the parkrun dream.

Sodbridge

The footbridge takes two abreast but being
Considerate of other users, we
Run single file—sensible when seeing
How the laws of natural frequency
Combined with mechanical resonance
Could cause our bridge a horrible mischance.

A trampoline will bounce you up and down.
Narrow footbridges on the other hand,
Have lateral and vertical renown
They wobble you, however well they're spanned.
To cross ours twice each Saturday invokes
Unease, passed off in mild suspension jokes.

History's littered with morbid stories of
Collapsing structures caused by soldiers who
Avoided breaking stride. Here, only love
Attends our parkrun crossings, but if you
Find up and down and sideways bridges odd,
This one, I can assure you, is a sod.

Ghost of Hillary

So soft and gentle on the outward lap,
The first climb is a doddle. The descent
Is where you make up for your handicap
Of age in what's mostly a young event.
Its slope suggests it might be heaven sent.

Try as you might to mentally prepare
You know that parkrun hill laughs at you when
You make the halfway turn. It's waiting there,
And twice as long and steep. You scale again,
Scoring it an eleven out of ten

For malice, spite, and purposeless revenge.
You invoke the ghost of Edmund Hillary
While feeling like a victim of Stonehenge.
You wish Sir Ed could make you more hill-ery,
Or at least be with you, your ancillary.

You've no breath to curse the monstrous mount.
Your eyes don't dare to contemplate its crest.
The steps required are tortures beyond count,
And yet you summit—you conquer Everest.
It's downhill now, the finish … and the rest.

Amateur pentameter

That fleeting passage in a run when time
Surrenders to a mindlessness of joy
Becomes a sort of worship. It's when I'm
Near godliness. My body's drugs destroy
My doubts and briefly I become a church,
Or vacuum, that suspends the ageless search
For meaning. So I work through my debate
Of will versus the sear and sneer of pain
And wonder when again
I'll have the chance to thus deliberate.

My run's rhythm is plain pentameter:
Two feet so purely central to the flow,
And iambs too. The rest is amateur.
It's true—the years have forced my pace to slow
And made me restless for my former youth.
Now, parkruns show a different sort of truth
In every pace and each relentless breath.
Endurance and humility now race,
Uncaring of a place,
But knowing they can run that race till death.

Discomfort zones

Have you noticed how every solid rule
Of human wisdom has a contradiction?
'Penny wise, pound foolish', for example,
Opposed by 'watch the pennies, and the pounds
Look after themselves'. Who would be the fool
To name one truth and brand the other fiction?
The evidence is in, dull but ample:
We're confused. Who should we trust? On what grounds?

My running past—cross country as a child,
The track, road races, and the marathons
That followed and consumed my days until
Age and fitness combined with fading time—
Caught up with me. So now my life's restyled.
Might I have slipped between discomfort zones?
The long, tough runs, once a matter of will,
Are shorter, but more regular, and I'm

Committed to the slower daily jog
That leads up to my parkrun Saturdays.
And here's the thing. So many in the race
Each weekend share one comprehensive aim:
To be or to become themselves. The slog
Unites us in our multitude of ways.
Me? Less mileage but somehow, still some pace.
The pain's no less. And I miss the distance game!

Spaced out on statistics

Statistics, data, information, facts—
The building blocks on which we base our lives.
They seem as certain as funerals, or tax.
What other subject actively contrives
To grab us when the parkrun post arrives?

The clock. Have I improved? A personal best?
No. I have to blame that extra glass of wine
Last night when I ought to have got more rest.
I went to bed feeling perfectly fine.
It's paid me back, but I've no cause to whine.

It's Saturday, the run's complete, and I'm
Afloat on a natural kind of drug.
Age, gender, place, and all-important time
Are screened, but I can shed them with a shrug,
Awash in my endorphin's glowing fug.

Running out of taxes

I got to fifty parkruns on the day
My tax year bottomed out its dismal trend.
My income seemed to match my feet of clay,
But unlike runs, the taxes never end.

So, groaning up our killer hill I thought
Just how the taxman might approach our race:
A duty on kilometres? A sort
Of GST levied on every pace?

Or worse, a surcharge on that prime essential —
A metered bill for every gasping breath?
Nothing could be more irreverential!
Athletes unite! We'll run ourselves to death!

Countdown to sub 24:00

Yes! At last you've shaved the awful seconds
Off that daunting target: sub 25:00
On your twenty fifth attempt. Glory beckons!
Hard work, soft winds, good people all contrive
To push you through. You're the gladdest man alive.

It's just a number on a stop-watch. Time,
That steady, incremental thief who picks
The pockets of our lives, still turns the crime
Back on its victims. It knows all the tricks.
You think you'll beat the clock? Watch how it ticks.

You'll take it just the same, knowing the run
Is no more than an individual test.
Your pulse tells you the countdown has begun
To shorter, slower races where your zest
Retreats before a cardiac arrest.

Results arrive. The evidence is clear.
You've made the PB you were anxious for.
It's done. Relax. You're finished. Quit the scene
And run for pleasure, no pain anymore.
Maybe. But imagine. Sub 24:00!

LORUS

SU MO TU WE TH FR SA

24:59:17

WATER 50M RESIST
CHRONOGRAPH

A run for all seasons

Scheduled the year through,
Even at the equator,
Seasons ebb and flow.

Should running alter
With cyclical change? Keep on,
Although you falter.

Summer

Heat and thirst and sweat:
The standard ingredients
Of a summer run.

With water at hand,
Gladness is a currency
In precious demand.

Autumn

Suppose autumn spoke.
Funeral leaves would whisper
Under runners' feet.

Hear autumn rejoice.
Our children's and runners' shoes
Liberate its voice.

Winter

Plumes of steam escape
parkrunners' lips and nostrils.
Air is visible.

Run through the winter
In training for the vintage
And you, the vintner.

Spring

A hide-and-seek child
Quivering to be discovered.
Winter won't give up

Until athletes throng
Spring's pulsating parks and paths,
Panting running's song.

Smart money

My local parkrun has its ups and downs.
I'm confident its elevation would
Persuade seasoned runners that even clowns
(Well, clowns like me, it should be understood)
Could conquer it with little beneath the hood.

Three hills with two sides each, deceptive slopes
Rise up then fall, always in that order.
They've flattish in-betweens to swell my hopes.
Here's terrain that surely should afford a
Guerrilla raid across my PB's border.

Six hikes, six drops. The first is an attack
On foothills less than Himalayas. I'm
At the front with youngsters, but hold back.
I never mix it with them on the climb.
I know they'll fade. It's just a matter of time.

I let them go and smirk my way downhill.
Five more peaks, and another five descents
Will leave me all I need to prove my will.
They spend youthful pounds; I save wisdom's pence.
My strategy makes fundamental sense.

Another hill. My theory starts to bend.
Ascent Three looms and I'm not making ground.
Don't panic. Hold your nerve. It's not the end.
I wish that Winston Churchill was around
To give me hope when only doubts abound.

Halfway, and I've abandoned all my plans.
Lungs, legs, heart, brain: each a mortal rival.
The black hole of my suffering expands.
Forget the clock, I'm clinging to survival.
The finish feels like Dead On Arrival.

parkrun people with Finish flags rejoice
As if we were Phidippides and cheer
Us with an undiscriminating voice.
Had I the breath, I'd gasp: 'I'm glad you're here.'
Next time I think I should just volunteer.

Newtrition

Some call me old-fashioned,
Some think I'm a freak.
When it comes to nutrition
I wonder each week

Could I boost my performance
With protein and gels?
I follow the experts
But each of them dwells

On their sponsored products.
Whichever one sells
The most at the check-outs
Rings advocates' bells.

I went back to Sheehan,
A doctor of note
On running, and he said:
'Not one gets my vote.'

Back to fasting it is
Like a hospital diet.
My run times improved.
I cannot deny it.

But I'm now at a plateau;
No PB in sight.
With parkrun tomorrow,
What's for dinner tonight?

The rogue

I'm here because I've picked a bloody fight
Against a rival every Saturday.
The question's pain, the answer is delight.

The course is marked, the marshal's out of sight.
The run director claims we're here to play.
I'm here because I've picked a bloody fight.

All ages, sizes, genders come despite
Embarrassment or suffering. They say
The question's pain, the answer is delight.

It does my head in. Am I wrong or right?
And why this fearful combat anyway?
I'm here because I've picked a bloody fight.

I know this foe who haunts me Friday night
Then drives me from my bed when I should stay.
The question's pain, the answer is delight.

That rogue is me. Resist with all my might
The start line's there. I cannot run away.
I'm here because I've picked a bloody fight.
The question's pain, the answer is delight.

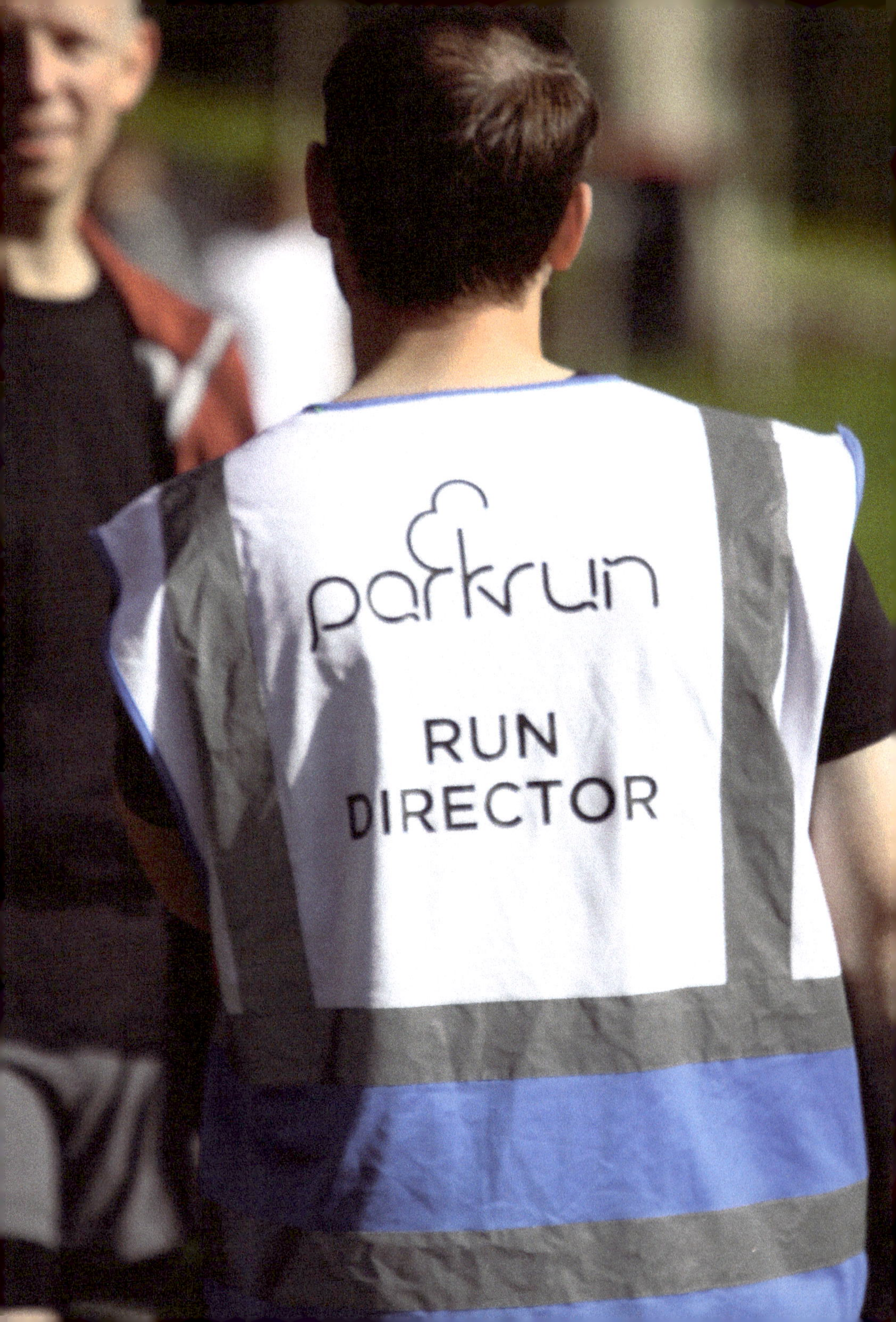
parkrun
RUN
DIRECTOR

Pop guns and top guns

The racer, the ambler,
The sprinter, the snail,
The dasher, the rambler,
The eagle, the quail.

The hero, the villain,
The hacker, the freak,
The flogger, the victim,
The shambles, the chic.

The hare and the tortoise,
The rabbit, the fox,
The crab and the porpoise,
The stallion, the ox.

The winner, the loser,
The ribbon, the cup,
The giver, the user,
The down and the up.

The butcher, the baker,
The hand and the glove,
The lover, forsaker,
The hawk and the dove.

The lion, the leopard,
The tiger, the lynx,
The sheep and the shepherd,
The camel, the sphinx

The monster, the insect,
The boxer, the beast,
The subject, the object,
The famine, the feast

Are all in our parkruns.
Some might be obsessed.
The pop guns and top guns,
All equally blessed.

Stopwatch conspiracy

My stopwatch is a tyrant.
It aids my deadly foe.
And time's a fire hydrant.
I cannot stop its flow.

My timepiece speaks a monologue
As simple as a brick.
We cannot have a dialogue.
It gets the final tick.

My stop watch is monotonous,
A second at a time.
Its purpose is lobotomous.
It's careless as a crime.

It tortures me in seconds,
Then minutes and then hours.
It's biased, though it reckons
It's neutral in its powers.

I don't do conspiracy.
The theory's anodyne.
Still … there is an intimacy
with parkrun's clock and mine

Origins. Is this tattoo for life?

That makes me think collusion
Can't always be dismissed.
This is my conclusion
Each time a PB's missed.

I know that time is justice.
I see that time is truth.
A question, and it's just this:
How come time favours youth?

Yes, it's age that now assails
Pride's need for flattery.
But next time that my stopwatch fails,
Forget the battery.

Battles with the lizard

'First twenty six, then twenty five;
You've shaved two minutes off.
How much longer till you arrive
At something like enough?'

My lizard brain—ape-man in me
That regulates my fear
And points out every enemy—
Was chirping in my ear.

'Remember when you almost said
You'd finished with PBs?
Having suffered, and having bled,
Is your parkrun disease

'Actually an addiction,
Destroying mind and limb?
My duty's your protection.'
I had to answer him.

I pointed out the parkrun race
Was not a race at all.
Personal bests were simply pace
Lines penned up on a wall

Barcode Tattoo

Like children's heights marked in pencil
On birthdays down the years;
A poignant, historic stencil
Of progress in arrears.

The lizard hissed and lashed his tail.
A million years unwound.
His ancient eyes glared rank betrayal.
He fumed. I held my ground.

Lizard and I have signed a truce.
He guards my week-day mind.
Come parkrunday though, I cut loose.
The reptile stays behind.

Sighchology

The bell curve of youth rears like a mountain.
No wonder it's also named a fountain.
In running terms, its sharp ascent is like
Jet fighters taking off, a vertical spike.

Just recently a stick-limbed youngster smashed
Our parkrun record. He left us ancients trashed.
Yet modest—shy—he was the epitome
Of running in every term permitted me.

The head, the heart, the body, and the mind:
Four complex concepts that we often find
Work contrary to one another and
absorb our dreams like water into sand.

We pant up hills, we run the roads and parks
Pursued by age extinguishing our sparks.
We jog the paths and flex to exercises
To staunch time and sanitise surprises.

Time calls to mind the grace of champions past
And present; those who burn and those who last.
Does it all come down to biology?
Age wonders if it's more sighchology.

Quick questions for slow runners

Is it wise to be so obsessed with time?
To run and watch your watch and sing or curse?
To feel your run's a victory, or a crime?
A triumph, or disaster? Better, worse?
Which comes first—the effort or the speed?
Is the creed a need, a deed, a greed?

You used to ask these questions of yourself.
The answers, when you found them, told you how
You wouldn't be left parked on running's shelf;
That you were fully present here and now.
The run became religion, you the priest.
Like some religions, understanding ceased.

It's best to solve these queries in reverse.
Easy said when the years have given you
Some hindsight, though you'll never beat the hearse.
One last question. When time has driven you,
What's left to learn? parkrun's response is plain:
Time is what you give, not what you gain.

First timers

I never thought that I was sentimental.
I always felt that logic ruled my brain.
Emotion is purely incidental
I told myself. I think those views remain
Except for Saturdays at parkruns where
Shy first timers are stunned by our applause.
I'm also stunned, having to declare
A loyalty to something like a cause.
Most movements and communities have been
Strangers to me, the solitary guy.
Now I read a global tribe between
The lines of parkrun, knowing somehow I
Can see the tale and ought to try to tell it.
Oh dear! Have I turned into a zealot?

Last shuffle

After fifty—that's parkruns, not my years
Which top that number by a cruel amount—
A recognition's set in. It appears
I may have reached a plateau. I'll be blunt.
The flame of PBs which I'd hoped to kindle
Has lost its spark; it's begun to dwindle.
As each event concludes, there's the feeling
That getting home under twenty three minutes
Is beyond my limits.
I've run up hard against my senior ceiling.

Should I accept my peak is in decline?
Admit performance seems a downward curve?
The injuries are fewer. I incline
To shorter distances, but where's the verve,
The steel nerves, the glacial killer instinct?
I ran my life wide-eyed, but now I've blinked.
It scarcely seems the time for slowing down
When others have no issue with the pace.
Must I settle for a place
When I've only ever chased the victor's crown?

The seasons spin remorselessly, and time
Is mindless, shapeless, careless, slow or fast
According to your circumstances. I'm
The average of my future and my past.
Does running slow time down, or move it quicker;
Intensify life's flame, or make it flicker?
What I know, have known since I was a boy,
Is gladness in movement and in muscle,
The ordered, lively bustle
Of mind and body fabricating joy.

Still, as life slows, as slow it must, I can
Take refuge in my memories hoping that
the ledger shows I gave my parkrun clan
a hearty tonk, a full swing of the bat.
There I go again, mixing metaphors.
Is this the evidence that semaphores
That drab descent from flat-out sprint to walk?
Pray I greet it with humour and with grace
And have the strength to face
My last shuffle bravely, and do not baulk.

Making up the numbers

I shouldn't be too clever when it comes
To mathematics. I failed my first test
At eight. I couldn't separate the sums
From equations, despite my tearful best.
I knew I'd reached my low numerical crest.

My only connective joy with numbers
Was running. I'd track each surging minute.
A dreaming stop-watch timed all my slumbers.
I was dawn's race, eager to begin it;
A one-boy fan club urging me to win it.

All has changed. The numbers are a shadow.
The tens of thousands of miles fade behind.
Would I run them again? I'd be glad, though
I'd pay a different toll on flesh and mind.
Now parkrun shows I can, if I'm inclined.

Time was a war

This trilogy of minutes was my countdown:
First twenty six, twenty five, then twenty four.
I wore them like a boxer's satin gown.
(Well, in my mind. It's just a metaphor.
Performance needs analogies, and more.)

The gown hid a yearning for improvement.
Time was a war. However well you fought
A failed PB felt like a bereavement,
And I'd run far too many of that sort.
How gaping the gulf dividing won and nought.

Some better shoes, a different strategy
With food and drink, a fresh approach to slopes
Might make a triumph out of tragedy.
I wondered how a flagging spirit copes
When only disappointment feeds its hopes.

I settled for a slower start and took
The first uphill thoughtfully and gently.
My foe, the stop-watch, never got a look
Until the finish where, eventfully,
I discovered that I'd done a twenty three.

Time was a marathon ago. Now I
Have learned the consequences of my pace.
I know it's more important that I try
For effort's sake and not to win a race,
But be content to know I have a place.

Forgot-me-knot

I see it almost every parkrunday.
The run director's briefing covers all
The issues you'd expect to come across:
A wobbly bridge, damp autumn leaves, the stray
Leash-less dog on the wrong side of the maul,
Fast cyclists, frost, a patch of greasy moss.

The risk they miss—it grips me in its thrall—
Is one all kids sooner or later face.
So plain, the slowest sporting folk still get it,
But with junior athletes, something seems to stall.
No idea? I mean the lowly shoelace.
D'you know how many youngsters still forget it?

That flapping string can sometimes prompt a fall
Or at the very least an urgent pause.
It's something most racers would rather not
Confront when answering their next PB's call.
Do you want to help parkrun's cause, and yours?
Some lace advice: just tie a double knot.

Blood running

A sonnet for the Stoics

We sometimes suffer for our sport. I mean
The niggles and the injuries that we
Endure on any given run between
Start and finish. It's like philosophy.
The Stoics understood. A muscle strain,
A trip and bloodied fall, a hamstring tweak
Was inconvenience instead of pain.
It might restrict their parkrun for a week.
I like to think I could be a Stoic
And earn myself a name for fortitude.
It wouldn't need anything too heroic;
Just a shift in my mental ought-to-tude.
So, I've been working hard to improve it.
Here's some evidence I feel will prove it.

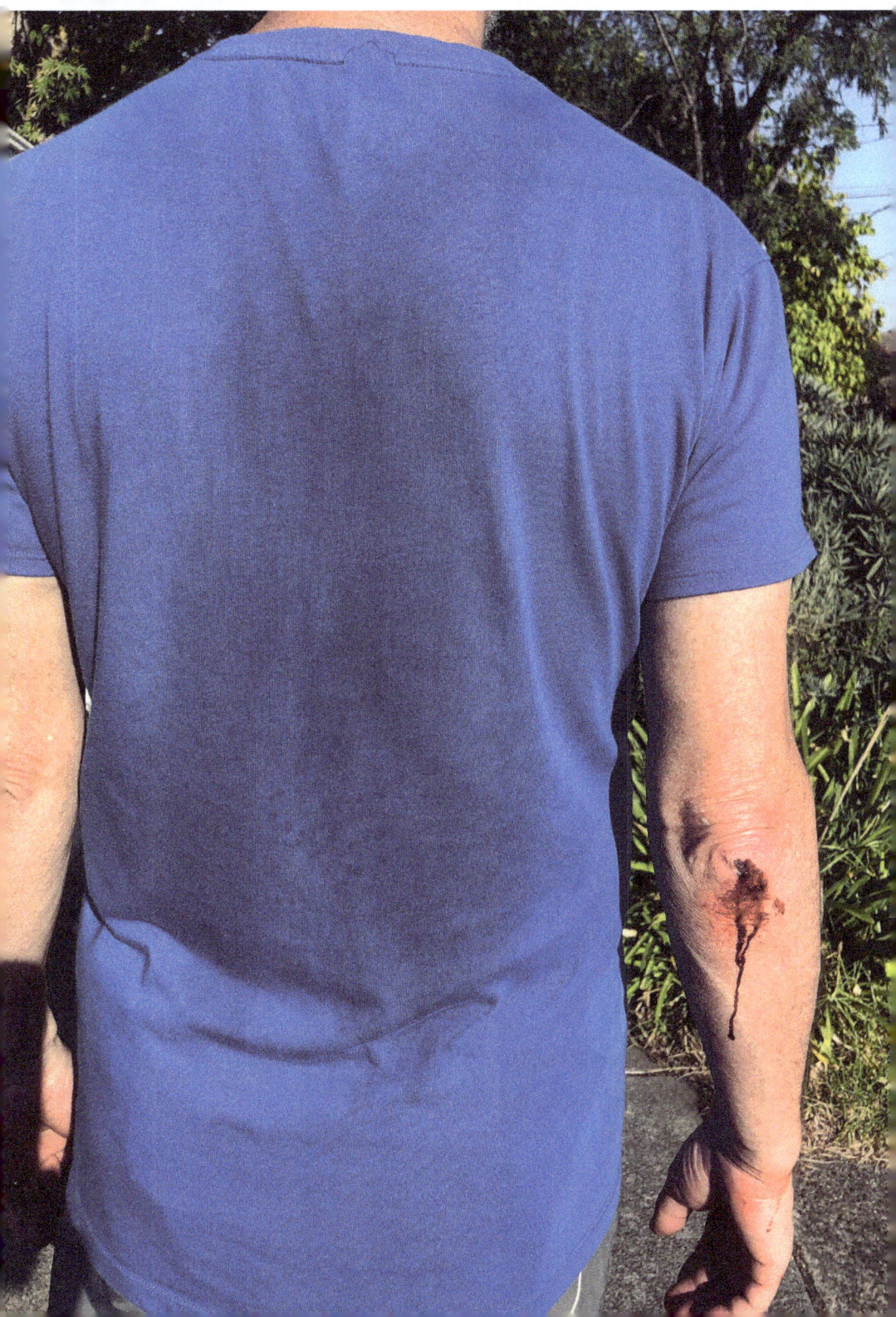

Chariots of childhood

It's rare to see a stroller in the lead.
By stroller I mean buggy, or a pram,
Or other wheeled device. These days the breed
Performs its mighty work from plain to glam
On three wheels or on four for extra torque,
And all who push display the same resolve.
Though some run, others are content to walk
And take the opportunity to solve
A worldly issue with a local chat.
These chariots of childhood symbolise
The parkrun parent as a democrat
And carer for whom children are the prize.
Push on. Your toddlers soak in all they see.
Absorbing life, in time they'll too run free.

Rain

Repeating motif.
In oppressive temperatures,
Vertical relief.

A blood-warm shower
During a tropical run
Restores some power.

Then it's winter's ire,
Hanging a lacerating
Curtain of barbed wire.

Wind

Invisible wall,
Like a hand-off to your face.
No point running tall.

Hot, it roasts your brain.
Cold, it minimises parts
Voiceless to complain.

Turn, and you attack,
An unexpected friend at
Your indebted back.

Smoke

This lung-provoking
Blue miasma reminds me
I gave up smoking

Thirty eight years back.
Bushfire fog from leagues away
Seeps to the attack.

A frosted-glass sun
Can't expel the bilious haze
Poisoning our run.

Snow

The sky has no tongue
But breathes out the dialect
Of an ice-carved lung.

What is its colour?
Why is its distance so bruised?
Could it be duller?

Air's a pillow fight.
Feathers on the run drift through
Heaviness of light.

Heat

You shiver with dread.
Horizons are mirages
Beckoning the dead.

They do not yet know
They could be walking corpses
Either fast or slow.

The wise turn away.
Why melt like an ice-cream cone?
Run another day.

Sweat

Running in glasses,
People categorise you
Within two classes.

To be called four-eyes
Can mean you're stupid, or wise.
Both are a surprise.

Either way, I sweat.
My spectacles slip when wet—
My runner's regret.

Humidity

It's like wading through
A sea of molasses,
And breathing it too.

Every inward gasp
Is the velvet-handled grate
Of a steam-forced rasp.

You'll never be cool
Nor understand why you played
Humidity's fool.

Sand

Brutal coaches tune
Their athletes, not just on sand,
But the savage dune.

Soft and giving sand
Is my eternal ruin.
It only looks grand

At a safe distance.
Few parkruns I know choose this
Point of difference.

Top ten

What do runners talk of when together?
Distances, times, their injury histories?
Or something more reflective, like the weather?
We're just like you, piqued by life's mysteries.

That August dawn, the rain had lashed all night.
I was soaked by a stormy bike-ride to
parkrun, its creek thundering in full flight.
Arriving saturated I spied few

Other runners grouped at the starting line.
It never crossed my mind the averages
Were on my side, not for a better time,
But better place. And over beverages

Shared at our local café I would learn
I'd worked myself into the run's top ten.
The weather-reduced field had helped me earn
A merit I may never reach again.

I look back on my eighth position in
The twenty two who braved the storm that day.
Pride fills my heart—yes, for my running kin—
But more for the volunteers who let us play.

A ton of running

One hundred. A ton of parkruns done. None won.
No victories, that is, against the field,
Just triumph over self when I'm the one
Most likely to roll over and to yield
To warmth and sleep when little else appealed.

Somehow I didn't, though I could have done.
Instead the pull of effort shared has made
The cold, the heat, the rain, and scorching sun
Complicit in joint suffering and swayed
Us back to be thoroughly parkrunday-ed.

Five hundred k's. How much of it was fun?
All start and end with chat and empathy;
The sense this thing could not now be undone,
and spread through a secret telepathy
Between the ranks of pain and sympathy.

The black T-shirt's long voyage has begun
From parkrun HQ. Now I look forward to
The teal two fifty top I hope will stun
parkrunners half my age or less, and who
aspire to the milestone. Wouldn't you?

CHAPTER 2

Volunteers. Winners come last.

Was it fate that I took part in my first parkrun on April Fool's Day? Was there any significance in April 1 2017 marking Coburg parkrun's one hundredth event?

Superstition and happenstance don't play a large role in my life. Lining up with just over 100 runners at the start line meant little to an old road runner like me. Pre-event banter in a community of athletes is the currency of running and racing. I expected nothing different here. But something unusual happened.

The run director gathered us for the start. Naïve me still thought it was a race. He drew a round of applause announcing Coburg's one hundredth event. He asked for a show of hands from first time parkrunners. I raised an arm, and so did a handful of others. To my surprise we were greeted with a hearty burst of applause and shouts and whistles of affirmation.

He then asked tourists—participants from other parkruns—for a hands-up. Another sprinkling of participants responded. Each was asked their parkrun of origin, and each received a warm ovation from the crowd. The further from Coburg, the louder and more appreciative the acclaim, especially if the visitor hailed from overseas.

Next, he thanked the volunteers individually by name and role. They were many: the director himself, pre-event course setup, time-keeper, finish token dispenser, barcode scanner, vision-impaired guide, photographer, tail-walker, and marshal. Each received an accolade.

All this for a struggle of amateurs (including me) over an unremarkable five kilometres? What was going on?

My first Coburg parkrun took an alternative route. Footpath and bridge maintenance on the southern part of the course forced the run north. From my training efforts in the months prior, I knew what to expect, except in reverse: mostly uphill out, and mostly downhill back.

The marshal at the half-way turnaround greeted us with as many variations of 'Well down, good work, keep going' as I'd ever heard. The photographer was a jack-in-a-box, in half a dozen places at the start and finish. The run director, time-keeper, and token dispenser at the finish line were a joyous and raucous reception committee. They made me feel like Pheidippides of Marathon for all the right reasons when I felt like that fated Greek for all the wrong ones. They still do.

By the time I had finished this book, I'd completed more than one hundred and fifty parkruns and volunteered scores of times in various roles. Why does the experience delight me as much as the welcome I received at my first parkrun?

Athletes know it as the runner's high. You might otherwise call it euphoria, contentment, happiness, satisfaction, the radiance of gratification that suffuses body and mind during and after a run. It's often masked by the stress, even the pain, of exertion. But it can paint an almost ridiculous grin on the faces of seasoned athletes and raw novices alike after the event.

All around it sit the three mostly insatiable human desires: to love, to be loved, and to belong. Few parkrunners plunge themselves into philosophical reveries like these as they pant towards the finish line.

But when my Saturday morning email inbox alerts me to the arrival of my Coburg parkrun results, a transformation occurs.

I see familiar names, a regular smattering of personal best times (PBs), the list of volunteers. Then there are the photographs reminding me of the miscellany of shapes, ages, sizes, and genders. And always among them, the hi-viz vests of the volunteers blaze out like neon beacons.

A flush of emotion—fellow-feeling, gratitude, tribal recognition—automatically washes through me. I belong, and not just to a small band of like-minded yet magnificently different enthusiasts. I know I belong to something much larger, an organism that uniquely celebrates me and every other parkunner on earth individually and collectively. And all made possible by the unspoken but universally understood code of the volunteer.

Winners come last

I am your parkrun tail-walker.
I follow up the field.
If you're an incessant talker;
If you don't like to yield

To loneliness on Saturdays,
Come to a parkrun 'race'.
It has become my latter days'
Focus in time and place.

Run or walk? It doesn't matter.
Prams and dogs and strollers
Add to the tail-end chatter.
We're not rock 'n' rollers.

My sometimes role is neither fast
Nor strenuous nor hard.
My duty is to come in last,
My singular regard,

Because all parkruns must protect
The health and safety of
Participants when they select
An act approaching love.

Enjoy yourselves; catch you later.
I've brought my phone along.
And here's our defibrillator
In case a heart goes wrong.

Barcode Tattoo

The finish without an end

Some search the running calendars, but know
No matter how we diarise, we won't
Quite get around to entering that race.
Excuses rule: too soon, too far away,
Too unprepared, too injured, just too slow,
The family may need us on that day.
We pencil the event, as is our wont,
Then make damned sure we're in another space.

But still, we do another search. What's this?
The parkrun entry crops up week on week
In unlikely places round Australia.
The quest reveals a local 5k run
A short bike ride away. Who could dismiss
A timed event where no-one is outdone
Except by self, and where the mild and meek
Can test their courage, *inter alia*?

We learn the power of the volunteer
Who, working with technology, befriends
The runners, walkers, children, prams, and dogs.
Bar codes and scanners work their magic and
A tail walker will patiently appear
With stragglers in a conversational band.
The run finishes, but it never ends.
If it were a machine, we'd be the cogs.

Running out of sight

'Don't forget, we're all in this together.
We're here to practice how to guide the blind
And VIs (vision impaired). Here's the tether.
It makes you and your mate two of a kind.

'So, let's experiment. Now, close your eyes
And hold this lead. We'll head off on our run.
Don't peep. Not once. You're in for a surprise.
Think blind. It could happen to anyone.'

Our teacher urged us out into the park.
I led hard, my partner uncomplaining.
How cool was this? Is running in the dark
That hard? A simple bit of training

And problem solved. 'Now swop.' You mean my turn?
I took the rope, and closed my eyes, and ran.
And hauntingly a shame began to burn.
For that moment, I joined the sight-dimmed clan

And stumbled into blackness at a pace
That, sighted, would have made me laugh. But now,
I'd given up my vision and my place
In my complacent world. And that is how

I learned a new and priceless courage though
It grew from a pretence and wasn't mine.
Blind runners and their guides don't care for show.
They humble me, and make our run divine.

Hymn of the parkrun marshal

At two degrees, it's warmer in my fridge.
The frost has icing-sugared trees and grass
And left a slick deposit on the bridge.
A runner could go over on her arse.

I'm blowing steam like smoking a cigar.
My fingertips (and other bits) are numb.
I'd rather I were in a cosy bar
Or café with a coffee. This is dumb!

Still, I am here. I guard the half-way cone.
I jog, but on the spot. I've a duty
To see through though I'm frozen to the bone.
My language is best described as fruity.

But here they come. Right on time. Both leaders
And followers pant their thanks. I'm impressed.
Compared to them, let me tell you, readers,
I'm almost indecently overdressed.

They smile and wave and turn for home and I'm
Made humble. Perhaps I could be partial
To braving this event another time,
For I am now a proud, new parkrun marshal.

Volunteers. Winners come last.

At the end

We steamed back through the cold, collecting cones,
Not from pines but the fluorescent ones
We use to mark our parkrun course each week.
I was marshal, he tail-walker. He spoke.

A magic tale strode with us in the mist.
It left me humbled, sanctified, and blessed.
No youngster I, he outdid me for age.
We'd traded greetings, always on the edge

Of faster, younger packs urgent to race
To better times. He seemed to be at peace
With pain and pace when the bulk of runners
Chase ever-finer, self-improving honours.

He'd come to running late, his partner dying
By degrees. Instead of life decaying
She urged him into celebration with
That regular run. Near her final breath

He promised her he'd dedicate himself
Not just to his but every runner's health.
And so he walked the tail to usher home
The stragglers so none would be alone.

Cone man

The witch's hats packed firmly on my back,
My two-wheeled steed attentive to my touch,
I cycle down Saturday's parkrun track.
I feel like a pathfinder with my clutch
Of cones: they seem so small, but mean so much.

New daylight seeps between the trees and creek.
I plant the first cone at the half way mark.
With map in hand, I pedal as I seek
Each fluoro beacon's locus in the park.
It's sacred work, and I'm the lucky clerk.

Novices and visitors rely on me
To find their way around a foreign course.
The marker cones are grace notes in a song we
Sing to welcome them to a global force.
If we're the parkrun pudding, they're the sauce.

The setup done, I'm ready for the run
And disappear back to the faithful ranks.
Our sacrificial ritual has begun
Though laughter makes it one of nature's pranks.
We thank the cone man. He in turn gives thanks.

fit FREE!

Free, weekly, 5km timed run/walk for all ages and abilities
Start/Finish: Coburg Lake Reserve, Lake Grove, Coburg

1. Register for **FREE** at www.parkrun.com.au/register
2. Print out your unique barcode
3. Turn up with your barcode, run or walk and have fun

Don't want to run or walk?
Help others by volunteering?

www.parkrun.com.au

The tailer's test

A four year old's just a puppy.
She wanders east and west.
Your compass growls: 'Please, south and north,
Not sideways; simply forth.'
The mind of a junior guppy
Looms as the tailer's test.

Your senior self grand-parently
Concedes that youngsters should
Enjoy parkrun's experience
Without your reticence.
Your tail-walk, apparently,
Can also do *you* good.

CHAPTER 3

Stories. Redemption through laughter and tears.

Like most enthusiasts, parkrunners talk. They also share stories. Many surprise themselves with the platform parkrun gives them to nurture us with heartfelt emotions they might otherwise never have expressed. The tales vary widely, as stories should. But some common elements constantly emerge. The parkrun pillars of community, collaboration, and encouragement shine through accounts of delight and dread, humour and hardship, privilege and pain, sickness and succour.

Fear is a recurring theme in many new parkrunners' stories. They reveal initial agonies of trepidation about their weight, ability, or appearance; of coming last; of looking foolish.

Other stories increasingly identify social and mental health issues. Socializing at even the most basic level for some is a struggle.

Heroic records of participation despite or because of a physical or intellectual disability make regular eye-moistening, throat-tightening appearances. In all these stories, parkrun is the linchpin, dealing with illness, accident, and misfortune. They humble us with their accounts of human resilience.

The latest frontier parkrun has crossed penetrates territory few other social movements could.

The often-dark world of incarceration rarely delivers redemption headlines. In the background, though, incremental improvements in society's approach to crime, punishment, and rehabilitation occasionally break through.

I've selected four original stories from parkrun history, from four countries. They seem to me to illustrate the spirit of parkrun in all its diversity. They remain exactly as they were published on their national websites: raw, tough, and yet warmingly redemptive tales of a simple idea touching and changing lives.

1. Prison break

The following story first appeared on the United Kingdom's parkrun website in March 2018. It had already created news around the UK, with stories presented by the BBC, ITV, and the *Guardian*.

'*Black Combe parkrun in Cumbria became the first parkrun event in the world to launch inside a prison on 4 November 2017.*

'*One of the participants that day was Alfy Kirkley who went on to complete 17 parkruns and set a new course record before his release last week. As he left, Alfy handed a letter to a fellow prisoner thanking him for introducing him to parkrun and promising to keep it up in the future.*

'*Alfy has asked that we share his letter publicly in the hope that it will encourage other prisons to consider starting a parkrun, and to show how the motivation of a weekly 5k event can have a transformational impact on anybody's health and wellbeing, whatever their circumstances.*

[The following letter contains some strong themes.]

'To Lee

'I don't do this often but I feel it's a duty or something more that needs recognition. I feel that you and Shane Spencer [Black Combe staffer and Event Director] saved my life and gave me hope when I was at a low point in my life.'

'I was at the brink of suicide at one point as I was trapped in a big hole, so what I would do in that situation was get high on drugs. I loved it, because it took me away from all my problems until I'd run out then bang, they would hit me again all at once. I'd then create problems not just for myself but for others too. I felt as though nobody could help me because they didn't understand my problem.

'I'll never forget when I met you. You came to my door and gave me the biggest bollocking ever – it came from nowhere. You told me I was worth more than that. I felt ashamed of myself but it sunk in and the penny dropped and you took me under your wing which I am grateful for. Not only that, you gave me self belief and self worth and got my head back on a level, not just physically but mentally as well, and I can't thank you enough for that.

'I've learnt a lot from you Lee and I've noticed that many others have too. You take time in helping people, especially vulnerable ones, when most people won't even take the chance and say hello or even look at you.

'I thank you for all the training you've taught me and I can honestly say it's paid off because one minute I was known as a jail junky and now all of a sudden I'm the fittest and fastest man in HMP Haverigg. I'm not just physically healthy, I'm mentally healthy and prepared for release and to continue this work out there. I feel a duty not to let you or Shane [Spencer] down so that's a promise. I will prove it.

'I can't thank you enough. I call you an honest, true friend and I'd definitely meet up with you out there and continue training and running – if you can keep up.

'So thank you again, take care and keep in touch mate.

'Your brother Alfy.'

2. How parkrun helped turn around an African tragedy

A second story, from the New Zealand parkrun website blog of October 14 2018, demonstrates the indomitable will of some humans. It's also a testimony to the the role parkrun played in re-building a life shattered by trauma.

'Sometimes one just has to wonder at the incredible will to survive and the strength of spirit some people possess—the following story by Graham about his father demonstrates this remarkably.'

'My 71 year old dad was attacked by a crocodile in South Africa at the beginning of the year. He had extensive injuries to his chest, leg and arms. His injuries were complicated by severe sepsis and required 18 operations, including an above knee amputation. After 42 days of intensive care, he was discharged to the ward and then eventually to [the] rehabilitation unit and finally home.

'Prior to the accident he was doing parkrun every week and it was a great incentive during his recovery and rehabilitation to get back and do it again. 'Indeed, I remember him mouthing "I'm going to get better and parkrun again" through his tracheostomy from his ICU bed, bandages and tubes everywhere. Our response was something like, "Erm, okay then".

'Recently he completed his first parkrun in Johannesburg with his new prosthesis. It took an hour and a half and he finished with blisters on his stump . . . but he made it step by step. It'll be the first of many.

'Family all over the world have started doing parkrun since then. Here in Auckland, my wife, kids and labrador manage to get to Cornwall Park most Saturdays and dedicate each completed parkrun to the strength it's taken with my dad's resilience and his positive attitude to life.'

Graham Knottenbelt, Cornwall Park parkrun, New Zealand

3. Living in the present

This story came from Gerry Stone, on Canada's parkrun blog in 2017.

'Up until 10 years ago I was a fit, healthy, happy, 45-year-old guy. I did triathlons, weight training, yoga, rowing and martial arts, and I was a circus performer too. Then in the blink of an eye my life was turned upside down and I was fighting for my life in hospital.

'A serious motorbike accident left me with a broken sternum, five broken ribs, a dislocated shoulder and a badly injured knee, back and hip. My left lung had been punctured by one of the broken ribs and the right lung was also very badly bruised. Shortly after the accident, both lungs failed and I began to slowly die.

'A doctor told my family that she knew of a machine called an ECMO machine that could possibly save my life. The machine is similar to the heart-lung by-pass machine used in open-heart surgery. It pumps and oxygenates a patient's blood outside the body, allowing the heart and lungs to rest. There were four of these machines at a heart/lung hospital in Leicester, but even if one of them was available my chance of surviving was only about 15%.

'As it turned out, three of the machines were being used to treat three special forces soldiers who had been injured in Afghanistan. So I was put in an ambulance and police escorted from Hereford to Leicester, placed in an induced coma, and connected to the machine for seven days. The machine essentially takes blood out of your body, oxygenates it, filters it, warms it up and returns it to your body, giving your lungs time to repair.

'The machine did its job, and four weeks later I was discharged from hospital. The hospital wanted to keep me in for another month but I wanted to go home. I was severely debilitated and struggled to do anything physically. I couldn't run, cycle, swim or lift weights – even walking was a major effort that left me breathless. I ballooned from a very fit 11 stone to 18 stone, I had very high blood pressure and on the verge of diabetes as a result I was suffering from severe depression. When I felt like I just couldn't take it any longer, one day I decided to take my own life.

'I'm not exactly sure what intervened that day, but shortly after leaving my daughter's house to find somewhere away from anyone I was struck down with a crippling bout of sciatica. I sunk onto all fours, turned myself around and slowly crawled the few hundred metres home. My PC was still on and my Facebook page was open, and on my newsfeed was the following quote by Lao Tzu:

'If you are depressed you are living in the past. If you are anxious you are living in the future. If you are at peace, you are living in the present.'

'I had studied psychology and had heard and read this quote many times, and it had never meant anything until that day. But in that moment I totally understood what it meant, and something clicked in my head. I began to sob loudly, then before I knew it I was laughing and crying at the same time. (I have now been a Buddhist for six years and in this time I have never felt suicidal again. I still feel sad and down sometimes, but this usually passes within an hour – the black dog has gone).

'As quickly as my life had been turned on its head, I resolved to do everything I could to rediscover my old self. I cut down to three small meals a day, started walking, then walk/jogging, then jogging, then running. Three months later I was six stone lighter, and that was when I mustered up the confidence to try parkrun.

'I had joined some running forums online and got talking to a local chap who told me about parkrun. He mentioned that Delamere parkrun was close to us, so I arranged to meet up with him and a few of his friends one Saturday morning. I was a little nervous and didn't know what to expect, as the last time I had ever run with anyone was when I was running at school. I stood at the start line and when the air horn blew I took off like a rocket, which was a big mistake! After 2k my legs started to die, and at around 4k there was a steep hill I had to walk up because my legs would not carry me. Once at the top however I ran the rest of the way to the finish, where my newfound friends were waiting and cheering me on. My time was about 40 minutes – a far cry from the 16 minute runner I had been years before – but the important thing was that it reignited my old competitive spirit and I was determined to improve. I had caught the bug.

'Everyone I met was so helpful and friendly and it inspired me to run more and to take part in as many parkruns as I could. parkrun has been a massive part of my recovery process – it has motivated me to get off the sofa and onto the streets, particularly when I started a job where I work on Saturdays and can't get to parkrun as often as I'd like. Over the following three years I worked really hard, adding yoga and strength work into my fitness programme. Then earlier this year I broke the magical 20 minute barrier at parkrun.

'But the best thing about parkrun for me has been the people I have met there. My fellow runners who encourage me, the volunteers who make it all happen, and the course marshals who cheer everyone along every step of the way. parkrun is a great place for all the family; two of my daughters, a couple of my grandchildren and one of my daughter's husbands have all started going regularly and they all love it. It's a great thing we can all do together, with three generations of the same family enjoying a healthy, sociable and, in my case, life-changing activity.

'My advice to anyone who has negative thoughts is not to dwell on them. If you sit there thinking about negative things you start to live them over and over again. I have turned my life around by living in the moment, and controlling my thoughts rather than letting them control me. I hope by sharing my story I can inspire and motivate others – whether that is to turn your life around or push yourself to achieve what you believe is impossible.'

Gerry Stone, Canada

4. Exercise as medicine

A final, noteworthy account of contending with life-threatening illness comes from the Australian parkrun website blog of May 17 2019.

'It has taken Frances Thompson three years to complete her 100th parkrun alongside her husband John. In between, she has had breast cancer, a double mastectomy, chemo and then last year multiple surgeries for breast reconstruction and for carpal tunnel in both wrists. She also had cochlear implant surgery, due to gradually going deaf in one ear.

'But during all that time, parkrun has been a constant for her…'

'My husband and I started doing parkrun in 2016 in Bendigo, Victoria and the volunteers and parkrun team were always supportive and encouraging when I came to parkrun during chemo or after I'd had surgery. Whether I was walking or doing a slow jog or being tailwalker I was always cheered on to the finish line.

'Several of my doctors told me they wished they could prescribe exercise instead of pills. Some people just want medication but don't realise that getting some exercise can help them better to get better.

'2017, a couple of weeks after mastectomy, just started chemo, not that unwell yet, so still managing to run

'For me, even when I was really unwell during chemo, getting out on a Saturday to get around a parkrun course made things not so bad, and the wonderful Bendigo volunteers kept me going. Chemo treatment makes your mouth taste bad, often a metallic taste. It gives you a brain fog and you feel lethargic. You are also bald, so that makes you feel self-conscious. But if I felt able to get up and get moving then walking didn't make me feel worse and being out in the park generally made me feel a bit better. Brisk walking means your salivary glands are a bit more active than if you are sitting still, and increased saliva meant I didn't notice the terrible taste in my mouth whilst I was up and moving. It certainly helped distract me from the misery of my situation.

'I wasn't supposed to be walking my dogs after mastectomy (major chest surgery means you can't put stress on your arms), but I worked out that I could connect a double lead to a waist belt, meaning hands-free daily walks for the dogs, out in the bush, where we were unlikely to encounter any other dogs.

'We then moved to Brisbane and our home parkrun is now Mansfield. Whilst I was having different surgeries I wasn't allowed to walk 5km, so I did a lot of volunteering. If you're new to an area, this also helps you get to know your area and meet new people.

'I've done 20 parkruns in Mansfield during the year that we have lived here, and during the various surgeries I've had in Brisbane, it has then been Mansfield vollies who have cheered me on and helped me get to the finish line.

'I've now recovered from my various surgeries, the cancer is gone and I feel so much better. I will probably never get back to my pre-cancer PB, but from my point of view, that really doesn't matter. It is really irrelevant whether I walk, run or shuffle. It doesn't matter what my speed is. I've got off the sofa and I am out in the park, getting some exercise.

'If you're bald due to chemo, get your Muslim friend to do a henna design on your bald head.

'I've got to 100 [parkruns], a half-deaf cancer survivor, who's not even a very good runner. My husband John is the fast runner in our family, always aiming to get under 24 minutes.

I'm thinking of aiming for an alphabet of parkruns next, and some overseas ones too when on holiday. And there are quite a few letter C parkruns around Brisbane, so I'm aiming to complete a pirate one as well (you need to sail seven seas and you need an arr . . .)'

Frances Thompson, Brisbane, Australia

Barcode Tattoo

Dream of freedom

Grey veterans and youngsters take their place.
The starting line will briefly hold them back
Until the timer sends them on their way.
Within that moment, energy and grace
Combine as nature's aphrodisiac.
Intention and innocence meet in play.

You marvel at the freedom of the run.
Air on your face, a rhythm and a pace;
Your body liberated, and your mind
A quietude that cannot be undone
Until you end the race that is no race;
The finish that re-links you to your kind.

Denial of the run, as prisons do,
Must be a sort of double torture for
The jailed, like zoo-locked creatures in their pound.
But mercy finds a way, and now a few
Reformatories have opened up a door
To parkrun as a means of making ground

Against bleak isolation and despair.
Some prisoners swear that parkrun gives them hope.
Others praise it for boosted self-esteem,
Connection to community, and care.
Not for them the felon's slippery slope.
They're running in pursuit of freedom's dream.

Stories. Redemption through laughter and tears.

The original Zambezi park run

A park, the bush, the game, a run, the friends.
This had them all. But wait for the surprise,
The kind only a running goddess sends.
It's Africa, and hidden killers' eyes
Burn from the bush. You wonder: 'Who's the prize?'

Two hundred thousand hectares crammed with game —
The big five—jumbo, lion, leopard, rhino
And buffalo. And thank you all the same,
A run's a run. Excuses? None that I know.
Some were worried. I knew I'd be fine though.

And off I ran, along the vast Zambezi
In midday heat, just for a treat, to say
I'd run through Zimbabwe. It was easy.
I didn't have to push through bush. The way
Was clear as day, I'd have to say, and hey!

The guides back in the camp had guns, and knew
The movements of the wildlife in the park.
The dirt beneath my feet was old and new—
An ancient dust, older than Noah's ark,
But fresh to me, the runner's ideal spark.

Barcode Tattoo

Acacias bloom, the river gleams, I zoom
Around a corner... headlong into farce.
Remember, it's Africa. With all that room,
How could any athlete of skill and class
Contrive to run straight up an elephant's arse?

The jumbo and I share bowel convulsions and
Skedaddle in opposite directions.
My first park run is not quite what I planned.
It's nineteen eighty three; parkrun's perfections
Are years off. Are they built on these reflections?

Each shared second

The armless trophy hides up on my shelf.
A little love and polish might return
Some former shine to my long distance self
And with it the endurance that I yearn
To re-discover when, an Under Nine,
I shared the athletes' cup with rival, Quinn.
A cross-country first, and it was mine;
A minor place, I'd have to halve the win.
For eight year olds, the course loomed up ahead
Enormously, beginning with a hill.
A dread of failure swamped my childish head.
I swallowed second place's bitter pill.
Back then, only first and glory beckoned.
Now, parkruns breed respect for each shared second.

...a Preparatory
Athletics
... 9 Champion
(Equal)
Roger McDonald

Unofficial coach

Her stats tell all: she's half my age
And one third faster than my best.
We high-five on her homeward leg.
I've yet to reach the half way peg.
She's up top on the parkrun page
While I languish with all the rest.

As we followers stagger in
She runs back out to urge us on,
Applauding us as though she were
Our coach, with no-one to prefer—
Not young, not old, not fat, not thin—
Just us on our mind's marathon.

Stories. Redemption through laughter and tears.

Motion in poetry

I watch Mo Farah. Straight away I think
Of poetry with every fluid stride.
It's enough to turn a hack like me to drink.
On track or road, I have no place to hide.
Thank God for parkruns. I'm anonymous
Whenever I'm visiting another.
Think hippo. Your reasoning's synonymous—
I waddle along. I cause no bother
Until I'm home, then out my laptop comes.
I pour out odes, couplets, and villanelles
Almost as fast as Mohamed Farah runs.
(In poetry, athleticism dwells.)
And now, could you ever dream upon it,
I've just run out Sir Mo a parkrun sonnet!

Gallop poll

I may not be a Nielsen or a Gallup—
Opinion polling's after all a science—
But as I contemplate our parkrun gallop
I question if there might be an alliance
Between the genders, even an affiance.

The journo in me cannot quite resist
A sampling of impressions of the course.
I try to be objective. I insist
On balancing the sexes as my source.
The run's for joy and sharing, not remorse.

Men and women smile in common accord
On elevation, length, and scenery.
My exit poll says visitors adored
The creek, the track, the birds, the greenery.
Younger runners were in-betweenery.

All genders (these days more than two) heap praise
On volunteers, so willing and so few.
Fast conditions leave boys in a cheerful daze.
But—it's no surprise to intelligent you—
High on the list for girls? A decent loo.

How to beat Mona* the marathoner

I wouldn't be the first, nor likely, last.
But having watched his running exploits I'm
Convinced I'm with a scheming group who would
Enjoy a kind of odd, inverted blast.
In parkrun terms, it seems a furtive crime
To trounce a hero just because you could.

Conspiracies by nature have a victim,
A target that opponents would defeat
By any means. Mine's Steve Moneghetti.
Puzzled, you enquire, 'Why have you picked him?
Olympian, world medallist, elite
Athlete and advocate. And don't forget he

'Ambassadors for parkrun especially here
In home town Ballarat. What's wrong with you?'
I wink. I know Mona would understand.
Not just a runner, but a volunteer,
He dons the hi-viz as good parkies do
To give support. And that is why I've planned

To run in Ballarat one weekend he
Performs the tail walk role for all of us.
My cunning plan is ringing in my head.
I'll beat him! It's a parkrun guarantee;
the price he'll pay for being generous.
(Nah. I'll walk with him. But end one step ahead!)

---

*   Steve 'Mona' Moneghetti, Australian and international marathon legend and parkrun ambassador.

CHAPTER 4

Expansion. Running all over the world.

———————————

As I completed this book in 2022, parkrun had spread to twenty two countries. Despite the ravages of the COVID-19 pandemic, the probability of further expansion looks as close to certain as any prediction you can venture.

The movement's universally translated message makes it a magnet for travellers across the geographic and cultural spectrum. So popular has it become that tourists planning local and international travel actively seek parkrun events as the motivation for, or a prized component of their itinerary.

My first and, thanks to COVID-19, only international parkrun so far was in Italy's beautiful city, Firenze/Florence. My travel diary warmly recalls the late September 2018 occasion:

'The whole morning was a celebration and a joy. The run took in most of the park, large by most standards, on the banks of the Arno River. My run to the start, which I calculated was also five kilometres, was along a wide, smoothly-tarred avenue flanked by quiet roads …

'The trees were just beginning to turn for autumn. The temperature was perfect, without a zephyr of breeze.

'It just happened to be the Florence parkrun's first anniversary—shades of my first ever parkrun coinciding with Coburg parkrun's one hundredth event.

'An English woman directed the event. Her Italian was perfect and clearly full of jokes. Strangely, foreign visitors outnumbered Italians by around ten to one. They featured a large contingent of Brits, many touring in groups.

'Some had flown over just for the event, or for the weekend. A good handful of Aussies was present, and a sprinkling of other nationalities in a field of about eighty. We were a jovial bunch with much chatter and laughter and encouragement.

'The run was a two-lap course almost entirely on gravel and dirt, and about as flat as you can get. We ran through dappled sun and shade with the light occasionally illuminating motes of dust thrown up by our feet …

'At the end, home-baked muffins and an anniversary cake awaited all finishers. It felt special to be associated with parkrun, and to belong.'

Expansion. Running all over the world.

Behind the parkrun curtain

Comrades! Years ago, the Iron Curtain
Was lifted and our nuclear IBMs
No longer made obliteration certain,
Just less likely. (Though with Trump and Putin,
Who can tell: our us's or your them's?)

I say with shame I cannot read Cyrillic.
My spoken Russian's merely *da* and *net*.
Competence in both would be idyllic.
Your history's oils, mine is still acrylic.
But here's a concept we should not forget.

We have a common language, and we speak
It Saturdays in special parkrun tongues.
Does it commence or finish off your week?
When will you give your last PB a tweak?
What's Russian for rubber legs and burning lungs?

I think of you, far comrades, as we run,
Each one of us challenging our gremlins:
Your biting snow and here, our brutal sun,
In parks through mud and dust till we are one
In running's churches, parliaments, and kremlins.

Great, Britain!

Unlike a few too many Aussies, I
Admire you Brits. I'm named for one of yours:
The Bannister whose pace proved so handy
At four laps of the track, and showed our Landy
A cleanish pair of heels. So let's give pause
To recognise the UK's sporting record.
Peter Ustinov put it amply by
Reminding us on sport's invention board

That Britain has a head start on the field.
Take cricket, football, rugby, hockey, golf,
And countless others; Poms have led the way.
You came to colonise, and stayed to play.
And when the natives bridged the sporting gulf
You simply conjured up another game.
Your sense of decent play has long appealed.
Without you, games might never be the same.

I see you chaps have pulled it off again
With parkrun. It's simplicity defined,
Democratising land, and health, and air.
I think of English parks when I ran there.
Fond but solitary memories flood my mind,
Though this time in the company of folk
Who take the *run* seriously but then
See the *race* as just a glorious joke.

Expansion. Running all over the world.

Long road to Canada

Your forests, mountains, plains defy
Explanation.
Like us, you're an almost empty nation.
Your mostly urban people congregate
Along your southern border. So would I
In preference to your frozen real estate.

You do a kind of cold like we do heat—
Beyond belief.
Your winters, our summers: trials with rare relief.
Much more connects us: language, Commonwealth;
A war history that overcame defeat;
A worldly view on dignity and health;

A largely friendly neighbour who
Shares with us all
The swift response to running's every call.
Your parkrun groups are flourishing, and I,
Down here in Aussie, have a run or two
To do before I end my race and die.

A parkrun in your Canada
Would be the aim
To reach before I pull out of the game.
Perhaps beside a river or a lake,
Could there be a better place to add a
New chapter to my life, for running's sake?

Time machine

We Mexicans, (from south of Queensland)
Have named it Surface Paradise:
A jewel tortured to a brand
Of plush slums on a sun-starved beach
Over-shadowed by greed and vice.
I pray my boyhood hero, Clarke,
Was miles beyond its grasping reach,
A mayoral candle in the dark.

I would rather remember Ron
As running's perfect time machine.
World record ace, he left upon
Athletics an immortal mark.
Oiled motion, he was pure and clean,
His triumphs dazzling as the sun.
How right he blessed that Gold Coast park
as parkrun's first Australian run.

Expansion. Running all over the world.

Copenhagen

In memory of Jens Staurup

Your Danish life has whispered to its end
Far from home, and far away from me.
We shared Australian space, and could pretend
A worldliness through games, the kind where we
Couch-bonded in a sports diplomacy.

In '91, the rugby world cup saw
Us introduced. Our partners read their books.
The broadcasts overnight exposed our flaw,
Earning us disapproving wifely looks.
Spent bottles brought us even worse rebukes.

Rare days. You knew your history. We'd talk
Of war, and politics, and when we last
Loved Africa, where we matured. We'd walk
Around your local lake in future past,
Alternately expectant and aghast.

And now you're gone. This country claims your bones.
But I run on, still in an adventure
No longer ours. The future makes no loans
When life's been foreclosed on by dementia.
Can there be a darker form of censure?

We gloried in ideas. I have one now.
Your Copenhagen hosts parkruns and I,
A stranger to your homeland, make this vow:
I'll run for you if I can get there by
My race's end. Till then, my friend, goodbye.

Fine *footings* in France

Debate about the primacy of language
Has raged across the centuries and will
Continue as long as French and English
Argue who's the bread and who's the sandwich.
I bear neither lingo any ill-will.
Should we speak *Franglais*, or chat in *Frenglish*?

This much I know: our parkruns speak all tongues
In many countries by speaking only one.
They need no special voice. Collective breath
Choirs it in a symphony of lungs:
The universal mystery of the run
That marks an active life from static death.

I doubt that your *Académie* would bless
The thought that a run in French is *footing*.
I've checked this with my Gallic friends who say:
'A little more oblige and less noblesse.'
In France, parkrunners know that they are putting
Their best feet forward, and *footing's* here to stay.

Expansion. Running all over the world.

Flying Finns

In running annals a tiny nation stands
Almost alone for records, heroes, gongs.
Sing of Kenya, Ethiopia, England.
Each land of runners eternally belongs
On pedestals. But don't forget small Finland.

What other country constantly demands
Olympic kudos for its athletes who
Became the ageless Flying Finns, a term we
Still delight in applying—breathless—to
Viren and the matchless Paavo Nurmi.

A Finland parkrun features in my plans
As every parkrun should while I still live.
Will I run Tampere? Heaven knows!
But I know that Tampere will forgive
Me if I don't before my earthly close.

Ode to German joy

Politics and history: those fatal friends
Conspired over centuries to turn
Your genius awry. But history ends
More often with a lesson all can learn,
A truth Deutschland would never lightly spurn.

Eight German parkruns. Doubtless there'll be more.
Less-travelled me has yet to visit you.
Organisation is what you're famous for;
Efficiency and technology too.
What else do your German parkruns do?

What customs do you follow pre- and post
Each event to keep your tribes together?
I imagine coffee would be the most
Sought after treat in your Teutonic weather.
Could I join you, whenever, wherever?

Expansion. Running all over the world.

Torn in the USA

You'll read this but the numbers won't make sense.
American enthusiasm sprints
Ahead of history, and my present tense
Is straight away your past. In my defence,
This parkrun thing's become a marvel since

Those funny Brits invented it back when
This century was only four years old.
You're up to twenty four events but then
That's just today, and when we count again,
Who knows the total? Might I be so bold

As to predict a flood of runners who
In time will get the message and turn up
In droves on Saturdays? It's what you do
When an idea is ready to follow through.
Your fans will surge as fast as Galen Rupp.

If I could choose a US parkrun, which
Would I select as my first choice and why?
The thought of running all makes muscles twitch.
No single one could satisfy the itch
Before I face that parkrun in the sky.

See how they run

It's not the kind of club you'd want your kids
To sign up to, but millions do each year.
You'll thank their stars it's not as cruel as SIDS.
But read this and I'll try to make it clear
Why you may have another role to play
Beyond our every parkrun Saturday.

See how we run. Confident. Clumsy. Fat.
Deranged. Encouraged. Skinny. Terrified.
Under-prepared or injured, hoping that
Whichever way it ends, we'll have defied
Our demons and breached the finishing line.
Ambition and ambivalence entwine.

What if the run represented something
Larger than us but microscopic in
Its focus, and we permitted nothing
To distract us? I have a topic in
My heart with which you will identify.
It's enough to make every runner cry.

That kiddies' club? The Club Foot curse that steals
Mobility from children everywhere.
Our project's in Zimbabwe* and the deal's
Plain brutal: thousands there lack basic care.
Untreated, they'll scarcely walk, and never run.
I wouldn't wish that fate on anyone.

Expansion. Running all over the world.

Search Ponseti. The fix is modest, neat,
And let's the child regain some precious ground.
It's momentum, reversing the retreat
Zim forced on them before they were around.
You can help. You needn't be a prophet.
Spread this book. We're sharing out the profit.

---

* CreateCare Global (CCG) is an Australian charity that supports orphans and vulnerable children wherever they are. A portion of the proceeds from the sale of this book goes to CCG and ZANE's (Zimbabwe: A National Emergency) Club Foot project in Zimbabwe.

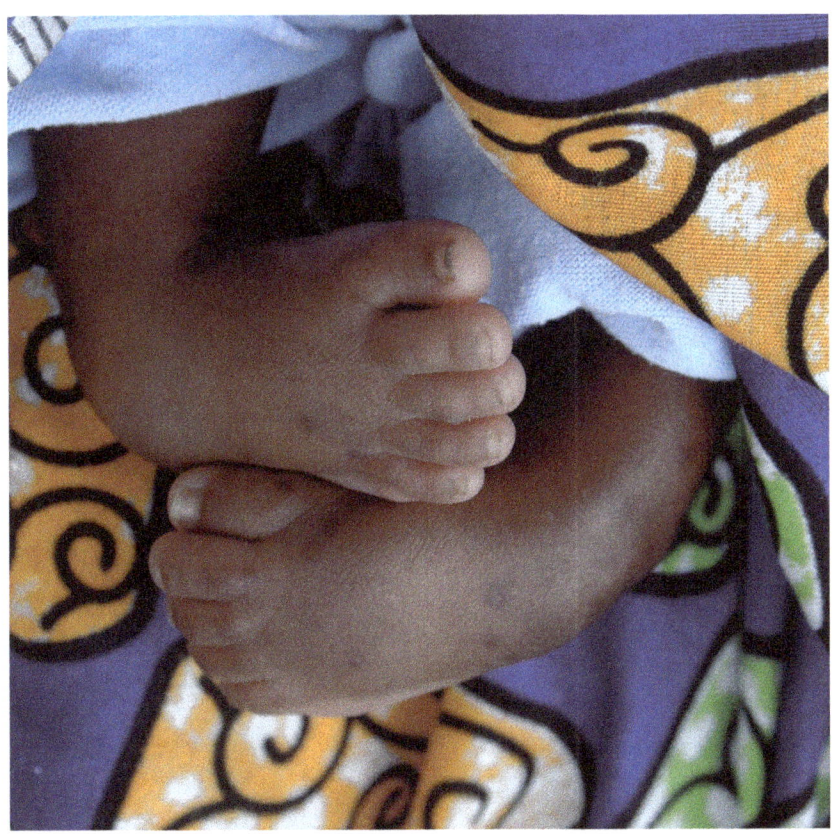

Garibaldi and my redshirt

One day I'll get to visit Italy.
I'll take my fifty parkruns shirt along.
Its red might be for Garibaldi's pride,
The fifty for persistence and for strength.
Maybe I can run it, literally,
The *Piazza del Duomo's* total length.
I'll jog through theatre, opera, and song;
Me and history striding side by side.

Two Bushy Parks

Not exactly a run, more an amble.
The running craze was scarcely underway.
I couldn't understand the mad attraction.

I'd always run, when boyhood poverty
Enriched you with shortages of choices.
Simplicity never got in the way.

Exhilaration needed no deposit.
Cross-country races called for no account.
They paid their dividends and interest,

One in beauty, the other in romance.
I couldn't know two Bushy Parks would bring
Their differences together in my life.

The original at Hampton Court, the scene
Of my amble in the nineteen seventies,
Now parkrun's birthplace and its spiritual home.

Bushy Park, Eastern Cape, South Africa,
My wife's ancestral home, where we've paid homage
To predecessors for their ox treks north.

Two Bushy Parks, two pioneering fountains
Nourishing diversities of lives:
Joy in generations, joy in running.

Expansion. Running all over the world.

Socrates does parkrun

Today we're in the pack with Socrates,
The Greek road-runner … Sorry, it's a jest,
Another of my mediocrities
I've singled out and hope, soon, to arrest.
We all have flaws. By now you will have guessed

That mine is flippancy, the ill-timed joke,
When the moment demands more sober thought.
Normally, I'm the world's least funny bloke.
But gravity goads humour when it ought
Invite responses of the sombrest sort.

Now parkrun's shown a way to turn it round.
I end events, groaning but believing
I've rediscovered Socrates and found
Another of his truths so worth retrieving:
'The unexamined life is not worth living.'

Ireland, a homecoming

Does any land have more myths and fables
And emigrants, heroes, and tragedies
That weave their way into so many histories
To share in stories round so many tables?
Ireland, one of my seductive mysteries.

One side of my Australian family came
From your jade land, the county of Kilkenny.
Today it sports a parkrun, and of any
Course I had to choose, I'd select the same.
Ancestry makes a tough choice over many.

Your running legends live, and you adore them.
They sprang, Irish brilliance from Irish loam
That sent its sons and daughters off to roam.
Perhaps parkrun can help to restore them.
If I could run there, it would feel like home.

Expansion. Running all over the world.

Eswatini, a kingdom for a course

I never made it to your borders though
Zimbabwe became my adopted home.
South Africa, so vast, so wealthy and
So dominant, surrounded you. And so
I never got there and therefore I must roam
Corridors of regret. Still, I have planned,

If only in my head, to make it to
Every parkrun on earth, no matter where,
Nor whether poor, middle-class, or larney.
We share the dream, and if we take it to
Dreams' extremes I might one day run there
On your rainbow course in Mbabane.

Holding a torch for Japan

No Olympic games
In twenty twenty's summer,
But hope still remains.

Summer twenty one
May yet deliver the games
And their rising sun.

Winter gloom will fade
And spring and summer complete
A glorious trade.

And if not, parkrun
Will bring fresh consolation
To everyone.

Postscript: brilliant sport
Proved twenty twenty one
Was no afterthought.

Expansion. Running all over the world.

Fantasia in Malaysia

Your tropical peninsula curves south
Like a finger stretching for the equator.
Geography like yours can make my mouth
A dribbling, drooling, tourist's salivator.

I must confess with some timidity,
One factor that concerns me is the climate.
Rain, hail, and shine, I'm fine. Humidity?
My runner's worst—a mountain. Should I climb it?

Of course! And if I make it to Malaysia
I'll make a point of tackling it head on
Though it may feel like ten rounds with Joe Frazier.
(Except, of course, that I'll still have my head on.)

The rest of me I'm not so sure. Perhaps
I'd take a bottle, sipping through the metres.
First, I'd seek advice from local chaps.
I'm told you sweat not spoonfuls, but whole litres.

The seven thirty start's a warning sign
That days heat up pronto in Malaysia;
A good excuse to walk the morning I'm
Dripping my parkrun dream in South East Asia.

Under Namibia's sun

I knew you—South West Africa—when you
Were struggling for your independence in
The last decades of the past century.
Poverty's still rife and resources few.
HIV/AIDS tests your resilience in
A place that for some's a penitentiary.

And yet your African spirit thrives on joy.
We see it in your attitude to sport.
Those who know could see the great day coming
When parkrun would welcome every girl and boy
And dreaming adult who in freedom sought
The solace and the sustenance of running.

In four years you've assembled four events.
And though your country's vast, its desert spaces
Beckon us whose blood instinct's to run.
More parkruns in your broad expanse make sense.
I can feel the pride in all those faces
Joined in running under Namibia's sun.

Expansion. Running all over the world.

Back from the brink

We know that parkrun is the people's race.
Fact: it is not a race at all but more
A mirror look at personality;
A self-analysis beyond your face,
Probing deep into who you were before,
And what might be your new reality.

All countries must be different. So time
And place and circumstance and populace
Ensure unique experience for all.
South Africa at one point was sublime,
But mostly for a white metropolis
And rural few who owned apartheid's stall.

Among them, though, were dissidents whose vice
Was opposition, in the open or
Beneath the surface, like rust under paint.
Of the former, remember your Bruce Fordyce
Whose black armband was Comrades' open door
To re-thinking apartheid's deadly taint.

Like all parkrun leaders, he takes no credit
For bringing his Rainbow Nation the event.
He says the people at large deserve a pat
On their collective back. Let history edit
The story of how, together, they present
parkrun's promise, and how they sport its hat.

Poland proves a point

You were in there early: twenty eleven,
With just five starters in Gdynia that day.
How in Polish autumn did you leaven
Their spirits when all others stayed away?

Whatever it was, the recipe has worked.
As I write, you're number sixth on the list
Of world events. Are bigger nations irked?
No. They know Polish courage, and resist

Temptations to draw comparisons when
Histories and wars always prove otherwise.
Do we need the past and all that went on then?
Yes, if we are to escape it, and grow wise

As Poles have done for centuries and show
Through parkrun your embrace of truth and health.
You've had your share of tragedy, but know
To move together is your common wealth.

Expansion. Running all over the world.

Kiwi dream

Is it fair to name names when so many
Among so few have covered you in glory?
Or talk of pounds when just a lonely penny
Was all you had to fund your running story?
Here's a truth—this is the kind of score we

Hold up to be the measure of the worth
Of small New Zealand on the sporting stage.
Consistently first, second, third, or fourth
On track, with ball, between wickets, no page
Lacks Kiwi Blacks or Silvers in every age.

Out of doors in the world's most outdoors place,
Your Tasman and Pacific islands form
Their splendid backdrops to the parkrun race.
It's not a race, of course, but the pure, warm,
And global dream you've made the Kiwi norm.

Who puts the Eden into Sweden?

An Aussie friend in Malmo says your place
Is paradise, the Eden of the north.
Though to my eyes, the photographs of snow
And runners cannot help but send a trace
Of nerves along my spine. Is running worth
That kind of sacrifice? Well, you would know.

I'm sure if I were there, and well-equipped
With all the clever winter gear you wear,
Your camaraderie would compensate,
With running's friendship added to the script.
Your gardens' and your forests' bracing air
Are bound to make me feel I'm on a date.

Who couldn't love your nation for its prize
Rewarding the noble with the Nobel?
Who next could win the world's award for health?
I know Stockholm must never recognise
Dull poets—empty churches with no bell.
But parkrun! Could it give us *wellth* by stealth?

Expansion. Running all over the world.

Foreverland in the Netherlands

I picture you: your polders and your dykes,
Your windmills and your tulips and your bikes
Retrieving freedom from your cities' roads,
Restoring cycling and running as the modes
Of preference to the transport-conscious Dutch.
From none in twenty twenty, now your clutch
Of parkruns has flown up to eleven
Making you a kind of runners' heaven
For a smaller nation. Blessed with a flat

And human-friendly landscape, I'll bet that
Canal and bike paths seethe on Saturdays.
Your runners, joggers, walkers—all ablaze
With friendliness—must see in each event
The goodliness of your country's intent.
No nation has three words that can describe
A Holland, Dutch, or Netherlandish tribe
Except you. May it last for ever and
Chime your name with parkrun's Foreverland.

High lights of Norway

Those Nordic names! Bergen, Grimstad, Oslo,
Stavanger and Trondheim, and soon another
Once again in Oslo. Then there's Tromso.
Your arctic town might one day be the mother
To the northernmost parkrun. How we hope so.

Imagine running in a midnight sun,
Or through aurora borealis' lights:
Panoptic purples, ghostly greens, silvers spun
Through stately stars at impossible heights.
My wonder is unearthed and re-begun.

Back to earth, your Nordic slopes and hills
Shrug shawls of snow across their shoulders and
Display indifference to runners' chills and spills.
What more of life could I wish to demand
Than this: one of Norway's ultimate thrills.

Expansion. Running all over the world.

Sing a song of Singapore

Your wealth and clout exceed most other countries
Many times your size and population.
Some sourly consider them effronteries,
As if land and people—in conflation—
Hefted them above your potent station.

But looking down the parkrun list I trace
Your presence proudly with your four events.
In your island city state where space
Is at a premium, who can make sense
Of parkruns in an urban place so dense

You are the third most crowded place on earth?
Throw the equator's steam into the mix
And we really begin to see your worth.
The freedom you promote is no quick fix.
Like running it involves no sleights or tricks,

Just honesty and effort and the sweat
Of locals and expatriates. Aligned,
They bring a message we cannot forget.
You're on my doorstep, close to top of mind.
Post-COVID? Let's run with you, sealed and signed.

Zimbabwe and the politics of running

When politics inserts its ugly snout
In people's lives, contending it improves
Their lot, it's certainly time to watch out.
You'll hear the needle stuck in falsehood's grooves,
And know it's time to search for other moves.

Despite the crimes, Zimbabwe was the first
Of all lands besides Great Britain to boast
A parkrun as the movement looked to burst
Beyond its boundaries. Many, if not most
parkrunners wouldn't know its founding host

Was Zimbabwe-born. Paul Sinton-Hewitt
Had his origins there. I'd like to think
That African running led him to it.
What's more important is its global link,
A miracle to which we all can drink.

My eight years in Zimbabwe let me run
Through innocence, before parkrun began.
Sadly, after politics quelled the sun,
Smothered by its Marxist bogeyman,
Sensitive people had no choice. They ran

Not for joy but for their lives, since cunning
And terror merge to masquerade as one.
Ah, politics—that loves opponents running
For borders at the barking of a gun.
When no-one's left to run, politics has won.

Running around Afghanistan

Does anyone truly win or lose a war?
Does conflict change the balance, or restore
Decency and justice according to
Some normal level while affording to
Each class and tribe the needs of their faction?
Can civil and military interaction
Bear fruit, or only bring about resentment;
Add rancour, or seed future contentment?
Who can tell? But an army on the ground
Might have an answer, if one could be found.

Camp Bastion, Afghanistan, was one
Where allied troops savoured their weekly run
With parkrun's structure proving a surprise.
Civilian staff and soldiers opened eyes
Around the parkrun world with times not seen
At any other run. They make me green
With envy considering their average
Was faster than my best. Was it a marriage
of fitness, discipline, determination
Bred on a sense of service to a nation?

Expansion. Running all over the world.

The military debate goes on forever.
Will we reach agreement? I think never.
It would be like asking hawks and doves
to—at the same time—share a pair of gloves.
Inside this conflict, parkrun found a place
Where combatants on one side could outpace
Themselves within their camaraderie
In search of Afghan peace as victory.
Risking death because it is your duty
Makes parkrun at your side a greater beauty.

Auden in Iceland

Despite its name, the island state of Iceland,
Is known by reputation as a nice land.
Its attitude is modern, culture decent,
And history—by Europe's standards—recent.
I first made my acquaintance with your island
Through a book I thought that I would trial and
Came back to over decades, not through boredom,
More a love of Louis MacNeice and Auden.
They visited in nineteen thirty six
And, up to all their literary tricks,
Play-acted as maestros and as phonies
While touring round your island on their ponies.

Their journey bequeathed us *Letters from Iceland*.
Their work is spiced with humour, sotto voce, and
A droll and dry wit suited to the north
Of anywhere provided you set forth
With honesty since Iceland has no sides.
According to Auden, classlessness abides
Like nowhere else. You'd think that ambit claim
Unwise of one already touched by fame.
Yet he returned in nineteen sixty four
And found he could re-iterate once more
His views—Icelandic light: the best on earth;
Equality, a native's gift at birth.

Expansion. Running all over the world.

What would Auden have made of parkrun if
He'd stumbled on it? 'Hardly worth a sniff,'
I hear him puff, taking a deeper drag
On his ever-present, lung-rattling fag.
'A lurch of lunatics obsessed with snow.
Have they nowhere in Iceland else to go?'
I say this from a distance when your parkrun
In Reykjavik has gone to the Dark One:
Black maths of geography and numbers.
Perhaps it isn't dead, but only slumbers.
As parkrun grows, momentum may return
To Iceland. You deserve a second turn.

CHAPTER 5

Tourism. Welcome, strangers.

One of the many attractions of parkrun is its consistency. No matter where you travel, if your destination has a parkrun, you know the format won't alter. And you have the reassurance that your results will be tracked and recorded just as they are at home, within hours or even minutes of completion.

Like all travellers, parkrun tourists have many and varied reasons for their adventures. Most simply like the thrill of the new: seeing unfamiliar places and meeting and making new acquaintances.

Others like to theme their challenges by all kinds of criteria: alphabetical, geographic, and numerical are just a few. These tend to be easier in countries where parkrun has multiple events in relatively close proximity. Distance, however, doesn't daunt the intrepid.

In my own country, Australia, we delight in travelling to or welcoming tourists from parkruns hundreds and often thousands of kilometres from home.

Many individuals, couples, and whole families make a rite of passage of circumnavigating the island continent by road. From the tropical north to the alpine south, many have begun to plan their journeys around parkruns, or at least include them in their itinerary. With nearly four hundred and fifty events currently at our disposal, we're spoiled for choice, of course. Reaching them all would be the work of a time- and money-rich zealot. Ah well, you can dream.

Pre-COVID-19, international visitors were a small but regular component of every Saturday. International vaccination programs remain our best hope for a renewal of these heart-warming pilgrimages.

Welcome, strangers

Some do it by the alphabet,
Some do it by the state,
Some do it by geography,
Or town, or name, or mate.
Some are visiting family
And some hope to create
An experience that might yet
Erase an old regret.

They represent the far and near.
Their numbers inch each week
Towards respectability.
You wonder if they seek
The same acceptability
That you chase as you creak
Towards a hope, away from fear?
Belief grows every year.

You sense it with each clap and cheer,
As loud for last as first.
You know you've found your worthy cause,
And how it slakes your thirst.
It's in the level of applause
For visitors. You've nursed
A dream, and speak it clear:
'Tourists are welcome here.'

Henry V at Darebin

A rugby girl (she'd grabbed a brother's shirt)
Lit the cold with a thousand watts of grin,
Shining me in to parkrun Darebin.
I wish I'd been more careful, more alert.
I might have caught her name before the gun,
But I was new and thought it was a race.
I learned it's not a contest, just a run.
Participating guarantees a place.

Odd that Darebin Creek, by which we ran,
Would, further south, meander past the school
That fifty years ago taught running's rule,
And where my slight athletic life began.
Today, though, names like CT Barling and
CH Sullivan—local worthies—mark
Our progress on the track. This happy band
Of brothers … sisters … ages … in their park.

Caught on the hop

This northern course, just 18ks away
From glass-bound sculptures soaring to the skies,
Will host your effort at parkrun today.
Suburban you expects no great surprise.

But you're amazed by strange bystanders who
Seem oddly shaped or ill equipped to run.
Few events have them. Nevertheless you
Choose tolerance in case things come undone.

Unlike your home course this is fast and flat.
Sandwiched between a freeway and parched paddocks,
It matches city parkruns' styles except that
This new element makes for a paradox.

What's one glitch to cause a parkrun upset?
Here's a peg on which you might hang a clue.
Although a matter now for amused regret,
You were outrun by a Lalor kangaroo.

Tourism. Welcome, strangers.

Sonnet for Florence

At last, a first! A parkrun in warm Florence.
I'd worked up to a full Italian frenzy.
The air lay still, azure poured down in torrents.
I'd flown the world to run in your Firenze.
I thought I'd be a stranger on the course,
The lone representative from Down Under,
But varied nations all turned out in force.
A dozen other Aussies stole my thunder,
Not to mention Germans, Brits, and Danes,
Americans, South Africans, and me.
Clearly, internationalism reigns
In this city and parkrun Italy.
No great surprise, when all roads lead to Rome.
I couldn't have felt any nearer home.

Farewell to Florence

Unmapped, I ran across Vespucci's bridge.
Viale dell'Aeronautica pulled me west
To *Parco delle Cascine's* foliage
And the Arno's banks, placid and caressed
By early autumn. In the sunflood, dust
From runners' footfalls rose on spot-lit beams.
An ancient time stood still as though a trust
Had formed between the stop-watch and my dreams.
The jog home took me past a Stars and Stripes.
A sentry with a side-arm threatened me
With foreign death. Australian me thought 'Cripes,
You need a parkrun, mate.' The enemy
Masquerades as ally? Farewell Florence.
You're perfect, but for that one small abhorrence.

Tourism. Welcome, strangers.

To beauty and to Bright

A first for you. Your jaunty hat
Declared you knew where all was at,
All being the sun about to shine
Whose scarring rays you must decline.
Some runners wore a baseball cap.
Others preferred the slip-slop-slap
Of block-out cream while still more went
Tit-for-tat-less, perhaps intent
On keeping down their racing weight.
That's my theory, at any rate.

Bright's run director welcomed you,
The sole first timer, a woman who
Found running something of a chore.
You'd walk this one to post a score.
A large part of the field was from
Distant parkruns far from home.
We tourists, confident that Bright
Would make the run our week's delight,
Flocked to the north-east town in scores
In search of running metaphors.

We also sought Bright's shades of autumn
And having found some, gladly bought 'em
With cameras and with eager eyes,
As thus I now soliloquize.
We began at Mystic Landing
The sixty-strong field soon expanding
Down Morse's Creek Road's rail trail
With you at first back in the tail.
The level footpath passed along
The creek towards Wandiligong

Through scrub, plantations, gentle farms,
And all Victoria's rural charms.
We gulped old air like new champagne,
The victors in a bold campaign
To run the world to better health
And physical and mental wealth.
Accustomed to my hill-packed course,
This flat track was a pie and sauce.
I sensed a brilliant run ahead,
All fear and inhibition shed.

Habit is such a subtle thief.
I knew by heart the parkrun brief
And set off for the half way cone
And hi-vis marshal there alone
To send us on our homeward way.
But there was no-one there that day.
I saw no runner turn around.
So on I ran and soon I found
My athlete's watch was telling me
I'd over-shot. Compellingly!

Retreat! I found the turn-round flag
I'd missed. I felt a proper dag.
At least I could alert you to
The missing marshal and (boo-hoo),
My lost shot at a new PB.
But now I sing a eulogy
To beauty and to Bright because
Combined they were the primal cause
That brought a once reluctant wife
To parkrun, and extended life.

Tourism. Welcome, strangers.

Happy for Lorne

Life-savers and their dinghies lined the beach.
A mountain-shrouding drizzle doused the flame
Of lesser running hardies keen to reach
The next rung on their inner ladder's fame.
Still, twenty five pitched up to play the game.

A pretty course embracing Loutit Bay,
The parkrun laps flow on the landward side
Of the world's largest ocean swim, they say.
Lorne's Pier to Pub is ocean swimming's pride:
Its Guinness record cannot be denied.

But I was there to run, having fought a
Battle with a cough, sore throat, and cold.
No swim for me. I'd sooner walk on water
Than plunge into the stuff and lose my hold
On sanity. I must be growing old.

Mid-way the rain cleared and a soothing blue
Seeped from waves in their own orderly race.
A turquoise mask, it had about it a hue
Of eye-shadow you'd expect on heaven's face.
More joy—I gasped my way to seventh place.

CHAPTER 6

Technology. Don't forget your barcode.

I know what it does, but how does it work? I'm a confessed Luddite. Part of me still lives in the age of quill and parchment.

But lest you think me a dolt, I easily grasp the concept of contemporary technology. How could I not? I carry in my pocket and wear on my wrist devices that would leave Dick Tracy swooning in envy.

What I struggle to master is their application. Not why do we have them, but how do I use them?

The title of this book is an acknowledgement of a bold idea and the extraordinary engineering that sits behind parkrun.

The original thinking of Paul Sinton-Hewitt and his band of pioneers—a free, timed, volunteer-led, exercise event open to everyone—seems in hindsight almost ridiculously simple.

Yet, from a fistful of hand-stamped metal washers, to smartphones scanning silicon barcodes, is a stupendous leap. Without doubt—and Paul Sinton-Hewitt's CBE is glowing testimony—parkrun has achieved two extraordinary feats. It has re-awakened a spirit of community well-being through outdoors activity, and given us the measures to enjoy, track, and share it like never before.

It's amusing that at the time of writing we still insist on parkrunners presenting a printed barcode at the finish to capture and record a time and place. I've no doubt the day is not far off when microchip applications or bio-technology will historically dismiss such measures.

Until that day arrives, don't forget your barcode!

Photophalia

If an image is worth a thousand words
I've just created half a million plus.
My parkrun photos stream like digital herds
From camera to computer: 'Look at us!'
They seem to beg, with me as their accomplice.

Out in the frost, my shutter finger froze.
But sports mode and a telephoto lens
Defied the ice and captured pose on pose
Of runners, walkers, kith, and kennel friends,
The lake, the birds, the run and all its trends.

At first a cold but soon a warming sun
Brought colour and comfort to a cheerful field;
Each photograph a glimpse of pain or fun,
Permanently and digitally sealed
In pixels all eager to be revealed.

The website tells the world how long the race took,
But photos are our online Kathmandu.
A web platform (did someone mention Facebook?)
Decided that my pix were no-can-do.
Such promise. Where's the techo follow-through?

Our best minds applied what-the-hecknology.
They plumbed the code of every useful app.
No matter how they pushed technology,
It couldn't fill the photographic gap.
As Larkin joked of books, it's a load of crap.

Technology. Don't forget your barcode.

Technical issues

I have joined the pantheon of runners
Who plot progress with a GPS device.
Now I too can revel in the wonders
Emerging from its digital advice.

I wear it on my athlete's wrist with pride.
It has all kinds of apps and screens and widgets
And who knows what other cleverness inside.
It gives me the speculative fidgets.

It talks to mobile phones and satellites.
It plays my tunes, pays bills, and claims to be
The prime source of every athlete's insights.
It may be. But why won't it speak to me?

This watch guides adventurers round the world
As they make their way, quick and whole-hearted.
You'll understand why I feel mildly churled
When I cannot get the damned thing started.

With it I'll go keener, faster, longer.
I feel a surge each time I strap it on.
I'm also sure I'd run a good deal stronger …
If only I knew how to turn it on.

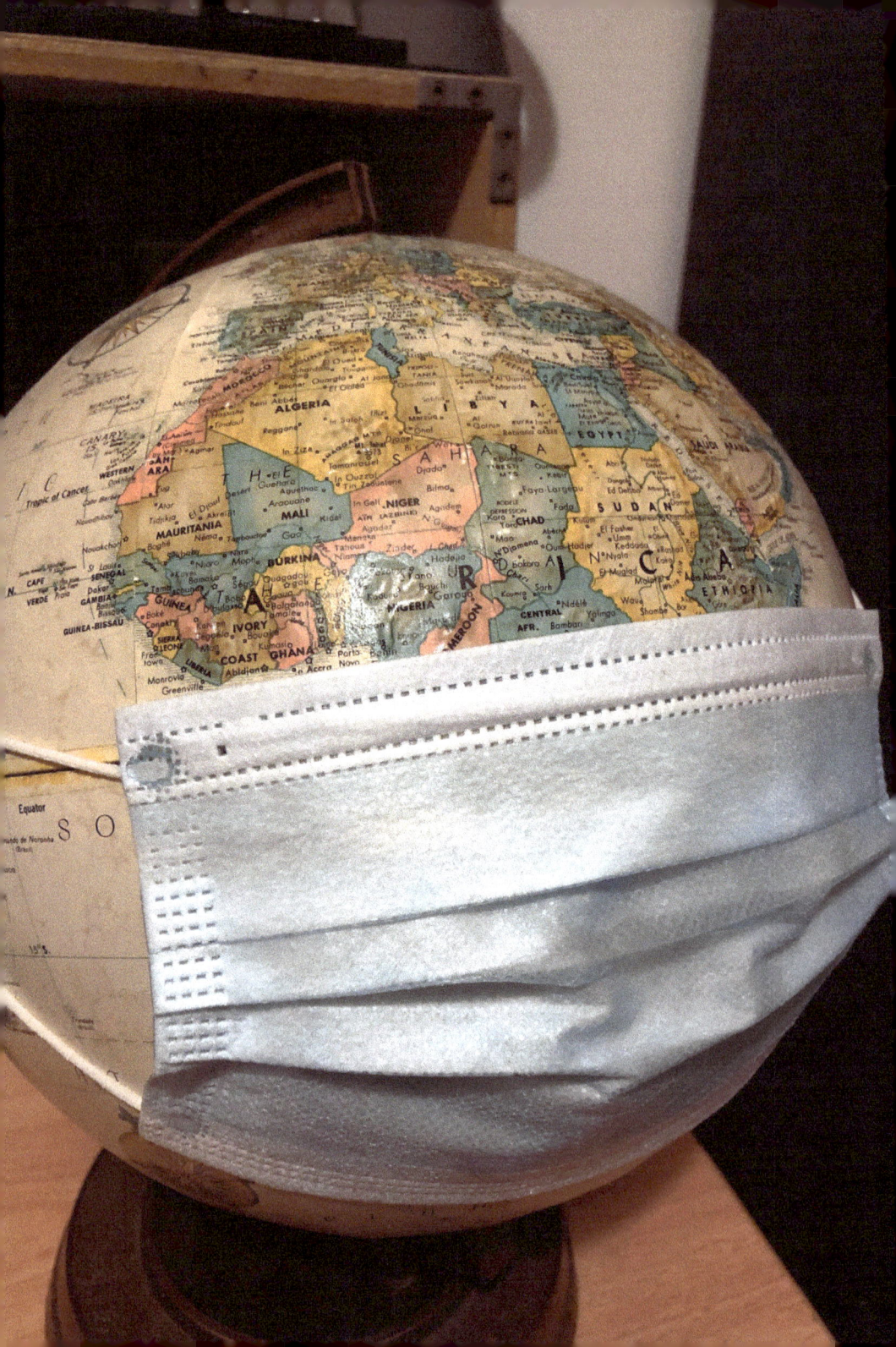

CHAPTER 7

Pandemic. COVID-19 and running on the spot.

From December 2020, the world reeled before the onslaught of COVID-19. The pandemic may not yet have been as deadly as other waves of pestilence in history. However, it shattered a global civilisation comparatively unscarred by a major contagion for a century and the impact of the so-called Spanish influenza in 1919 and 1920.

The economic and cultural impact of COVID proved unpredictably devastating. National and international borders closed. Millions were thrown out of work. Cities and states went into lockdown. Some jurisdictions declared and enforced curfews. Facemasks, once thought an unnecessary option, became mandatory. Queues for COVID tests lengthened.

'For the first time, the possibility of a parkrun cancellation due to corona virus was mentioned. Apparently, for the moment, public events attracting no more than 500 participants are immune (pun intended) to cancellation. But news unfolds hourly.' (My running diary, March 14 2020.)

A week later my running diary reveals a desultory message for parkrun that day. The entry declares:

'We received the now expected news via the Coburg parkrun website during the week. Sadly for the world's parkrunners, most countries have elected to fall into line with health authorities and parkrun international and cancel their events for the foreseeable future.'

Can a catastrophe of this magnitude bring any benefit, leave us with any lesson, or convey any comfort? I was luckier than most. My wife, Sandy and I had run our own business for decades. We were used to working from home.

The lockdowns and curfews limited our capacity to see or visit family and friends. But technology meant my writing and marketing and Sandy's business coaching could continue almost undisturbed.

The theory seemed incontestable. My clients disagreed. They obeyed the classic downturn knee-jerk theory—in uncertain times, cut the marketing budget first. My income plummeted by ninety per cent virtually overnight. Sandy's took a hammering too. The intervention of the Australian Government's JobKeeper program provided a welcome trickle of income, and the temporary suspension of mortgage and other payments relieved some of the burden.

Fortunately, the authorities took a positive position on exercise. At the deepest levels of lockdown in my home town, we were confined to home for all but one hour a day and could not travel outside a five kilometre radius from our residence.

However, outdoor exercise, including running and cycling, was still permitted. As a bonus, we were exempted from wearing a face mask, although still required to carry one.

Although my personal level of running dipped marginally, the lockdown and slump in business made more time available for other pursuits. So strange were the times that poetry seemed to spring naturally to the fore. One outcome was this book, *Barcode Tattoo*.

COVID closure

Bad pun, worse news, all parkrunners' bombshell.
Our event—and the world's—was not immune
To COVID cancellation. Who could tell
How long the ban would last. A few weeks? Soon,
In days not weeks, Corona's true extent
Imposed its spiteful presence on the globe.
What demonic agent could invent
Something as satanic as this microbe?
Three weeks became 'till further notice' then
'Indefinitely' as the virus spread.
We grieved first timers, the child's milestone ten,
And other achievers forced to watch their thread
Snapped, with no return to fix their eyes on.
COVID's wrath imposed a bleak horizon.

Save your breath

The lockdowns were almost universal
As cases and deaths climbed up through clouds.
Lack of reaction too was controversial.
Some countries thought immunity of crowds
Might just work if they simply went along
With business as normal. What could parkrun do
But minimise the risk? I thought it strong,
Courageous leadership; who would undo
A strategy that must have saved the lives
Of millions who might have caught the virus?
Until a safely proved vaccine arrives
We won't have parkun here to inspire us.
Better that than compromised health, or death.
Running is how we want to spend our breath.

Pandemic. COVID-19 and running on the spot.

Back from the dead

It's on, at last! Almost a year has fled.
A cautious crowd (a crowd no less) creeps back.
We're Lazarus, returning from the dead,
Survivors of this odd viral attack.
We keep our distance, promise not to spit
Or blast snot shots from our phlegmy nostrils.
We groan: 'Who'd have thought? Can we still do it?'
We greet friendly faces like fond apostles.
The run director's brief is circumscribed;
Short welcomes for first timers and for tourists.
The volunteers aren't named, the course described
Too briefly for the liking of the purists.
But we're alive and COVID hasn't won.
At least this round is ours. And we can run.

The Covid Chronicles

Twenty twenty and twenty twenty one
Declared they were something extra special
For many wrong reasons. But they've begun
To liberate our spirit; show the flesh'll
Hunker down, cry 'retreat' but not 'defeat'.
In record time, world-wide collaborations
Affirmed: 'This is the foe we have to beat.'
And did. And now global vaccinations
Seem possible. These two years gave us time
At home—the new workplace—to calmly look
At fresh ideas and ways of thinking. I'm
Glad to say I found space to write a book:
The Covid Chronicles: a work in verse—
The worst and best of COVID's random curse.

THE COVID CHRONICLES

ROGER G McDONALD

PAINTINGS BY CALLY LOTZ

CHAPTER 8

Future. Can yesterday ever be tomorrow?

Some of *Barcode Tattoo* was written shortly before the COVID-19 pandemic cast its uncaring shadow over the universe. As the scourge extended its deadly tentacles, my poet's heart bled for the death, damage, and sorrow it spread through unsuspecting communities.

I wrote another book, *The Covid Chronicles.*

I hope the back cover blurb summarises the book and the times it tries to capture:

'The microbe that stopped the Earth

'From toilet paper wars to lockdowns to global politics *The Covid Chronicles* gives you a commentary on the Covid-19 pandemic like none other.

'Written over the months of Australia's wave of lockdowns, the work reflects on the novel coronavirus that shut down the planet. The chronicles examine the origins and impacts of the contagion from its first outbreak in Wuhan, China, through the European crises, to the disaster in the US and a damaging jolt to its reputation on the world stage.

'Few aspects of the phenomenon escape its attention. Yet, for all the enormity of the deaths and casualties, the language is musical; hardly surprising when you consider the book consists of 100 Shakespearian sonnets.

'Fear not if you think you're about to face a tsunami of *Shall I compare thee to a summer's day?* Though the format takes advantage of an enduring classical structure, these are contemporary sound-bites. The metre skips along and the language is poignant, probing, and movingly funny in parts as it records our responses to the global event of a lifetime.

'Cally Lotz's luminous and evocative paintings complement the poetry to perfection. They pick out apparently simple motifs and invest them with an emotional intensity and symbolism rarely associated with everyday objects.

'*The Covid Chronicles* may not supply you a comprehensive history of a far-reaching event that affected most of humanity. But it will give you an enjoyable, easy-to-read, and touching reminder in the years ahead of life with Covid-19.'

The Covid Chronicles is a kind of diary in verse. It was my attempt at making sense of the first truly international trauma since the Second World War. I penned a sonnet a day for seventy five days until it seemed the worst of the crisis was over.

My timing was sadly awry. Inexperience, inefficiency, and plain ignorance saw new outbreaks of the virus, with more restrictions and lockdowns. I went back to my desk and wrote another twenty five sonnets, thinking a round hundred might have some cabbalistic effect. COVID didn't even shrug its shoulders.

One of the sonnets made a direct reference to parkrun and its ability to unite and bolster communities:

Retreat, not defeat

I wrote one time that running was my church.
The rhythm of the movement was my prayer
As I gasped on my introverted search
For selfish meaning, breathing greedy air.
I thought back then it clarified a mind
Already simple, stripping down to nought
My vanities outside of human-kind.
So foolish. Now I'm grateful parkrun taught
A clearer version of humility.
I've learned there are dividends in service;
That volunteering in community
Can bring about a metamorphosis.
Today, a deadly virus spells retreat.
Keep running. This will not end in defeat.

Although COVID forced parkrun to suspend its operations worldwide, its communications platform never closed. It sustained the belief that individuals and communities could overcome the most intrusive afflictions. And even though parkrun events couldn't congregate physically, parkrun invented means by which participants could maintain the faith.

It is now clear that the idea and the philosophy of parkrun has taken root for good in the world's imagination. With continually growing numbers, its future—and perhaps with it a small but significant part of the future of humanity—seems hugely more hopeful.

Double negative

Was I a traitor to the cause?
My double negative of not
Running new (not)parkruns because
The times felt as though they forgot
Our run, undid the binding knot,
And locked us in a year-long pause?

Of course I ran the lanes and roads,
Resorting sometimes to the track.
I noticed how an absence goads
A different effort when you lack
Familiar footsteps at your back.
I thought I'd lift my rate by loads.

I didn't quite. The COVID rules,
While sanctioning some exercise,
Were critically tough on schools
And businesses. No-one denies
Personal memory defies
Our recall of the odder jewels

The lockdowns thrust on all our days.
Our local curfew put a stop
To night-time training with the gaze
Of neighbours part-inclined to shop
You to the all-empowered cop;
5k limits; the face mask phase;

Future. Can yesterday ever be tomorrow?

And social distancing that made
Us lepers in the shops and streets.
Restrictions eased, we still evade
Our fellows lest history repeats
Infection from someone who greets
Too closely. Some still feel betrayed.

(Not)parkrun's chiselled in the books
Because it had to happen when
The course of events stops and looks
The other way. But not again,
I pray with a devout Amen,
Echoed—I hope—by other sooks.

Run for all, all for the run

It's brilliant to know that parkrun flourishes
In twenty two nations where it nourishes
A vast international tribe of souls
From millionaires to prisoners to proles.

Not all are runners; some are volunteers,
Supporters, carers, the friend who engineers
A broken mind or body back to life;
An anxious husband or despairing wife

Who, at wit's end or past their final grouse
Reconstitutes a sad, reluctant spouse.
These stories—and results—proliferate
Through parkrun's annals and accelerate

As week by month the global numbers grow.
The good news is devoted to the slow,
The shy, the awkward, the sensitive, who rise
To most excuses shunning exercise.

Reprieve lies in their reach if not their grasp
(as Browning and heaven knew) with that first gasp:
'Try running fifteen seconds, rest a minute.
Repeat your race for one. You can win it.'

Future. Can yesterday ever be tomorrow?

I scanned a list. My curiosity
Itched to discover whose ferocity
For health and sport topped the host of nations,
And who finished as the poor relations.

To measure, I took national populations
Divided by parkrun events. Equations
Emerged slowly. Giant calculations
Take time, but I expected no sensations.

Surely the guns—the US, Britain, Russia
Would lead the way? In their wake they'd usher
The next sports nuts who medal without failure:
New Zealand, Scandinavia, Australia.

You won't believe who tops the parkrun list.
(It's flawed, all statisticians will insist.)
It's not your London's, New York's, Moscow's, Auckland's,
But Port Stanley in the tiny Falklands.

What does it prove? Nothing and everything.
It demonstrates a plain idea can bring
A universal benefit to all:
At parkrun, even the least of us stands tall.

Index of titles

A

A run for all seasons	46
A ton of running	78
Amateur pentameter	38
At the end	89
Auden in Iceland	146
Autumn	46

B

Back from the brink	135
Back from the dead	171
Barcode Tattoo	25
Battles with the lizard	57
Behind the parkrun curtain	115
Blood running	68

C

Category of one	27
Caught on the hop	152
Chariots of childhood	71
Coburg molehill	30
Cone man	90
Copenhagen	119
Countdown to sub 24:00	44
COVID closure	169

D

Democracies of distance	33
Discomfort zones	39
Double negative	178
Dream of freedom	102

E

Each shared second	106
Eswatini, a kingdom for a course	131

Index of titles

F

Fantasia in Malaysia	133
Farewell to Florence	156
Fine *footings* in France	120
First timers	61
Flying Finns	121
Foreverland in the Netherlands	139
Forgot-me-knot	67

G

Gallop poll	110
Garibaldi and my red shirt	126
Ghost of Hillary	37
Great, Britain!	116

H

Hamstrung	28
Happy for Lorne	161
Heat	75
Henry V at Darebin	151
High lights of Norway	140
Holding a torch for Japan	132
How to beat Mona the marathoner	112
Humidity	76
Hymn of the parkrun marshal	88

I

Ireland, a homecoming	130

K

Kiwi dream	137

L

Last shuffle	63
Long road to Canada	117

M

Making up the numbers	65
Motion in poetry	109

N

Newtrition	50

O

Ode to German joy	122

P

Photophalia	164
Poland proves a point	136
Pop guns and top guns	53

Q

Quick questions for slow runners	60

R

Rain	72
Retreat, not defeat	177
Run for all, all for the run	180
Running around Afghanistan	144
Running out of sight	87
Running out of taxes	43

S

Sand	76
Save your breath	170
See how they run	124
Sighcology	59
Sing a song of Singapore	141
Smart money	48
Smoke	73
Snow	73
Socrates does parkrun	129
Sodbridge	34
Sonnet for Florence	155
Spaced out on statistics	40
Spring	47
Stopwatch conspiracy	54

Index of titles

Sub 25:00	26
Summer	46
Sweat	75

T

Technical issues	165
The Covid Chronicles	172
The finish without an end	86
The original Zambezi park run	103
The rogue	51
The tailer's test	92
Time machine	118
Time was a war	66
To beauty and to Bright	157
Top ten	77
Torn in the USA	123
Two Bushy Parks	128

U

Under Namibia's sun	134
Unofficial coach	108

W

Welcome, strangers	150
Who puts the Eden into Sweden?	138
Wind	72
Winners come last	84
Winter	47

Z

Zimbabwe and the politics of running	142

Index of first lines

A

A first for you. Your jaunty hat	157
A four year old's just a puppy.	92
A hide-and-seek child	47
A mist rises chilled off the surface.	30
A park, a run, the bush, the air, the friends.	103
A rugby girl (she'd grabbed a brother's shirt)	151
After fifty—that's parkruns, not my years	63
An Aussie friend in Malmo says your place	138
At last, a first! A parkrun in warm Florence.	155
At two degrees, it's warmer in my fridge.	88

B

Bad pun, worse news, all parkrunners' bombshell.	169
Brutal coaches tune	76

C

Comrades! Years ago, the Iron Curtain	115

D

Debate about the primacy of language	120
Despite its name, the island state of Iceland,	146
Does any land have more myths and fables	130
Does anyone truly win or lose a war?	144
'Don't forget, we're all in this together.	87

F

'First twenty six, then twenty five;	57

G

Grey veterans and youngsters take their place.	102

H

Have you noticed how every solid rule	39
Heat and thirst and sweat:	46
Her stats tell all: she's half my age	108
How many body parts can let you down	28

Index of first lines

I

I am your parkrun tail-walker.	84
I got to fifty parkruns on the day	43
I have joined the pantheon of runners	165
I knew you—South West Africa—when you	134
I may not be a Nielsen or a Gallup—	110
I never made it to your borders though	131
I never thought that I was sentimental.	61
I picture you: your polders and your dykes,	139
I see it almost every parkrunday.	67
I shouldn't be too clever when it comes	65
I watch Mo Farah. Straight away I think	109
I wouldn't be the first, nor likely, last.	12
I wrote one time that running was my church.	177
I'm here because I've picked a bloody fight	51
If an image is worth a thousand words	164
In running annals a tiny nation stands	121
Invisible wall,	72
Is it fair to name names when so many	137
Is it wise to be so obsessed with time?	60
It's brilliant to know that parkrun flourishes	180
It's like wading through	76
It's not the kind of club you'd want your kids	124
It's on, at last! Almost a year has fled.	171
It's rare to see a stroller in the lead.	71

L

Life-savers and their dinghies lined the beach.	161

M

My local parkrun has its ups and downs.	48
My stopwatch is a tyrant.	54

N

No Olympic games	132
Not exactly a run, more an amble.	128

O

One day I'll get to visit Italy.	126
One hundred. A ton of parkruns done. None won.	78

P

Plumes of steam escape	47
Politics and history: those fatal friends	122

R

Repeating motif.	72
Running in glasses,	75

S

Scheduled the year through,	46
So soft and gentle on the outward lap,	7
Some call me old-fashioned,	50
Some do it by the alphabet,	150
Some Saturdays, my email pats my back.	27
Some search the running calendars, but know	86
Statistics, data, information, facts—	40
Sub 25:00! Your mantra and nirvana	26
Suppose autumn spoke.	46

T

That fleeting passage in a run when time	38
The armless trophy hides up on my shelf.	106
The bell curve of youth rears like a mountain.	59
The footbridge takes two abreast but being	34
The lockdowns were almost universal	170
The racer, the ambler,	53
The sky has no tongue	73
The witch's hats packed firmly on my back,	90
This lung-provoking	73
This northern course, just 18ks away	152
This trilogy of minutes was my countdown:	66

Index of first lines

Those Nordic names! Bergen, Grimstad, Oslo,   140
Today we're in the pack with Socrates,   129
Twenty twenty and twenty twenty one   172

U

Unlike a few too many Aussies, I   116
Unmapped, I ran across Vespucci's bridge.   156

W

Was I a traitor to the cause?   178
We know that parkrun is the people's race.   135
We Mexicans, (from south of Queensland)   118
We share a passport like a striped tattoo   25
We sometimes suffer for our sport. I mean   68
We steamed back through the cold, collecting cones,   89
What do runners talk of when together?   77
When politics inserts its ugly snout   142

Y

Yes! At last you've shaved the awful seconds   44
You count the leaders until you make your turn.   33
You shiver with dread.   75
You were in there early: twenty eleven,   136
You'll read this but the numbers won't make sense.   123
Your Danish life has whispered to its end   119
Your forests, mountains, plains defy   117
Your tropical peninsula curves south   133
Your wealth and clout exceed most other countries   141

About Roger G McDonald

Poet, writer, journalist, editor, and runner, Roger G McDonald, was born and educated in Melbourne, Australia. He has lived and worked in New Zealand, the United Kingdom, France, and Africa.

His poetry first appeared in England in the 1970s. Since his return to Australia in the 1980s, many of Australia's leading newspapers, magazines, and literary journals have published his work.

They include The Age, The Australian, The Bulletin, Hobo, Island, Overland, Quadrant, Southerly, and Voices.

He is the author of multiple self-published and yet-to-be published collections of verse. Among them is a soon-to-be-completed collection devoted to the broader subject of running. He has also published extensively through social media.

His online poetry wins regular praise from other writers and social commentators.

Roger lives and works as a writer in Melbourne with his wife, Sandy, who is an author, TEDx speaker, artist, and story-telling teacher. Sandy designed and typeset both *Barcode Tattoo* and his previous book, *The Covid Chronicles,* published in March 2021.

They have two daughters and three grandchildren.

Other works by Roger G McDonald

The Covid Chonicles

From toilet paper wars to lockdowns to global politics *The Covid Chronicles* gives you a commentary on the Covid-19 pandemic like none other.

The work reflects on the novel coronavirus that shut down the planet.

Few aspects of the phenomenon escape its attention. Yet, for all the enormity of the deaths and casualties, the language is musical; hardly surprising when you consider the book consists of 100 Shakespearian sonnets.

The Covid Chronicles may not supply you a comprehensive history of a far-reaching event that affected most of humanity. But it will give you an enjoyable, easy-to-read, and touching reminder in the years ahead of life with Covid-19.

Heart Yarns

A tiny, disabled black South African orphan receiving a blanket from a middle aged white South African woman is hardly front page news, if news at all. Yet it has sparked a minor miracle. The miracle grows bigger by the day.

The work of knit-a-square.com for southern Africa's orphaned and vulnerable children has shown us love and care survive in our age of cynicism.

The response from the world of knitting and crochet—to a plea from knit-a-square.com to knit and send small squares to Africa to be sewn into blankets—remains astounding.

https://rogergmcdonald.com

You, parkrun, and the simple gift of soap

We left Zimbabwe to return to Australia in 1984 to escape the increasingly brutal regime of the tyrant, Robert Mugabe. We had very little, but at least we had our freedom. Australia has been immeasurably kind to us.

My Zimbabwe-born wife, Sandy, still carries a part of Africa in her blood. She founded a charity in 2008 after a visit from her South African aunt. She told us the combined perils of AIDS and extreme poverty in sub-Saharan Africa had orphaned or made vulnerable an estimated 25 million children.

CreateCare Global's purpose is to bring love, comfort, and warmth to orphaned and vulnerable children worldwide.

Since she launched the charity, one of the projects she has co-founded, **knit-a-square.com,** has seen around 20,000 crafters in more than 70 countries supply over 2.5 million squares to make an estimated 500,000 blankets.

A current pandemic-related project in Uganda supplies soap to orphanages and community carers who lack even this most basic item of hygiene. Please visit create-care-global.org to see the extraordinary work care-givers do for these often-desperate children. Would you then consider getting involved?

Part of the proceeds of the sale of this book will go to CreateCare Global and Zimbabwe a National Emergency (ZANE).

Thanks for your support—Roger and Sandy McDonald.

https//:smallacts.global

www.ingramcontent.com/pod-product-compliance
Lightning Source LLC
Chambersburg PA
CBHW062115290426
44110CB00023B/2819